SPIRITUAL GIFTS
REIMAGINED

SPIRITUAL GIFTS
REIMAGINED

The Journey View

BILL SMART

ILLUMIFY
MEDIA.COM

SPIRITUAL GIFTS
REIMAGINED

Copyright © 2023 by William J. Smart

All rights reserved. No part of this book may be reproduced in any form or by any means—whether electronic, digital, mechanical, or otherwise—without permission in writing from the publisher, except by a reviewer, who may quote brief passages in a review.

The views and opinions expressed in this book are those of the author and do not necessarily reflect the official policy or position of Illumify Media Global.

Unless otherwise indicated, Scripture quotations are taken from The Holy Bible, English Standard Version.® Copyright © 2001 by Crossway, a publishing ministry of Good News Publishers. Used by permission. All rights reserved.

Scripture quotations marked NIV are taken from the Holy Bible, New International Version.® Copyright © 1973, 1978, 1984, 2011 by Biblica, Inc.® Used by permission of Zondervan. All rights reserved worldwide.

Scripture quotations marked NASB are from the New American Standard Bible.® Copyright © 1960, 1962, 1963, 1968, 1971, 1972, 1973, 1975, 1977, 1995, 2020 by The Lockman Foundation. Used by permission.

Published by
Illumify Media Global
www.IllumifyMedia.com
"Let's bring your book to life!"

Library of Congress Control Number: 2023900395

Paperback ISBN: 978-1-959099-17-8

Typeset by Art Innovations (http://artinnovations.in/)
Cover design by Debbie Lewis

Printed in the United States of America

To My Wife, Susan, Who Is Carefree, Delightful, And Full Of Faith—Living *Agape* To Me.

To My Mentors: Margaret, Who Directed My Eyes To God's "Phenomenal" Work In People; And Robert, Who Validated Me In Serving Others "Subversively" In Love.

CONTENTS

Preface   ix
Acknowledgements   xiii
Introduction   xv

Part One: Take In The Panorama   **1**
Chapter One: Spectrum Of Grace   3
Chapter Two: The Spoils Journey   13
Chapter Three: Cross Wisdom   25
Chapter Four: Powerful Love   37

Part Two: Walk The Journey   **48**
Chapter Five: Imagine Your Inheritance   49
Chapter Six: Engage Your Battles   61
Chapter Seven: Be You Like Christ   74
Chapter Eight: Your Listening Community   86

Part Three: Strategies For Church And World   **98**
Chapter Nine: Values For Church—Teaching And Growth   99
Chapter Ten: Values For Church—Fellowship And Service   111
Chapter Eleven: All People Are Gifted   123

Part Four: Study The Concepts   **134**
Chapter Twelve: Three Views On Gifts   135
Chapter Thirteen: Interpretive Factors   145
Chapter Fourteen: Romans & Ephesians   157
Chapter Fifteen: 1 Corinthians & 1 Peter   168

Chapter Sixteen: Categories Vs Uniqueness	178
Chapter Seventeen: Manifestations Of The Spirit	190
Conclusion	197
Worksheet 1: Agape Evaluation	198
Worksheet 2: The Gifting Journey	207
Appendix 1: Propositional Summary	213
Appendix 2: The Spoils Theme	215
Appendix 3: Integration Issues	224
Endnotes	227
Reference List	251
About The Author	257

PREFACE

"Who can I get to serve in that role?"

I asked myself that question numerous times during my years as a pastor. My job? Pursue potential recruits and fill the position. In order to serve well, I needed to check off that task. In the ideal situation, securing a new church volunteer can be a wonderful experience for both the recruiter and the recruited. It feels rewarding to help someone find a fulfilling ministry match that powerfully uses their strengths to positively impact others' lives.

I filled many roles with recruits during my twenty years of pastoral ministry and twelve years of parachurch leadership. Filling positions fits the definition of success, right? It certainly kept me busy. But circumstances weren't always ideal.

Sometimes a person in a ministry role started displaying behaviors that revealed immaturity. Behaviors that interfered with their ability to effectively minister to people, often hurting others as a result. Maybe I had a good handle on that person's spiritual gifts as a fit for a role, but something was missing. I began to see that my job was not as simple as matching the right person to the right ministry.

I also wondered if successfully filling ministry roles, even with good matches, was really what Jesus had called me to do. Honestly, the task felt rather organizational. Was I simply helping to keep a machine running smoothly?

Certainly, the "machinery" of your church is a vehicle God uses to touch people's lives every day. But what about effectively helping people grow as disciples of Jesus? For a number of years, I was seeking to understand what it looked like for a church to disciple people. Meanwhile, though, roles still had to be filled.

I'm guessing you didn't pick up this book to learn about discipleship or spiritual growth. Perhaps you're wondering if there's a need for a fresh perspective on spiritual gifts. What you hold in your hands is a book that talks about both—a book that integrates gifts with growth.

Here's what happened to me. One day it dawned on me that neither Paul, with his longer and hard-to-categorize gift lists, nor Peter, with his super-short gift list, received these lists on stone tablets handed down from heaven. So I wondered, *How did they get those lists?*

That question propelled me into years of study on the topic of gifts. Out of that curiosity, an alternative point of view of what spiritual gifts are gradually emerged.

Another experience that happened to me is my own growth as Jesus' disciple. God blessed my journey with mentors and friends who helped me see the battles I needed to fight in order to grow. And guess where those battles were? In my heart. My heart is where I was scarred by sin and enslaved to fears and idols. Yet it was also the battlefield on which I needed to engage my foes.

As I went further along my journey of healing and growth, something wonderful developed. No doubt I was already using some of my gifts at some level. But the more I grew, the dormant and undeveloped gift potentials in me became unleashed and effective. The more secure and clear I became about who I am in Christ, the more I blossomed in gifted ministry. If I had not engaged the battles I needed to fight, I would not have realized my fuller gifted potential.

My biblical studies about gifts led me to conclude that spiritual gifts are not about things we get at a certain point in time. Instead, spiritual gifts speak of the beautiful diversity of the people God created and our unique journeys as we battle to discover and develop our gifts.

My own journey and my gift studies were harmonious in their messages. As time went on, I eventually found myself assisting in leading a personal growth workshop in which we supported people as they fought their heart's battles, and each one discovered their uniqueness as God's creation. They were moving further toward their full gifted potential.

If you are a pastor, I want to help you discover an understanding of spiritual gifts that addresses both how people are gifted to serve and where they are in their journeys of growth. If you are a Christian layperson, I want to inspire you to develop your gifted potential as you grow spiritually.

For churches, I want to invite us to grow in the wisdom and love that diversely gifted communities of people need to truly live as Christ's body. Finally, I want Christians to see that their unbelieving friends are also diversely gifted, and that this common ground forms a space for sharing Jesus.

ACKNOWLEDGEMENTS

Besides my wife and mentors whom I mention in the dedication, the following people impacted me along the journey that led to writing this book.

My parents, John and Mary Lee Smart, saw that from the cradle I was taught faith in God and faith in his Word. Their legacy persists within me. About thirty years ago, after hearing me share my thoughts about gifts, Dr. Warren Benson encouraged me to publish a book one day. I never forgot his words.

In recent years, I've been blessed by the close friendships of four brothers in Christ: John Houmes, Scott Stever, Greg Waldo, and Randal Weidenaar. They challenge me and love me. I have been strengthened by their encouragement and graciously helped by their feedback as I labored on this book.

I'm thankful to the team at Illumify Media Global for their wise and patient guidance as I developed this manuscript and prepared it for publication.

Now that I'm in my sixties, there are more people than I can list who have supported and shaped me. I feel very grateful that they've been in my life. Finally, I am grateful to the many people whom I served in various roles over the years. They trusted me to listen to their hearts and walk alongside them during some of their battles. Those experiences changed, grew, and deepened me.

INTRODUCTION

Spiritual gifts: We read the books, taught the classes, used the tests, debated the issues, and where did all that leave us? If you're a pastor or lay leader in a church, perhaps you're left with a mixture of thoughts and feelings when it comes to gifts . . .

- "We used to think it was strategic to help people figure out which gifts they have. But maybe it's not; we don't do it anymore. And we definitely don't want to focus on arguing about which gifts are still active today."
- "We teach that each person's need is to be connected with fellow believers, grow in Christ, and serve others in love. That seems more important than defining each gift and giving people tests so we can plug them into ministry roles."
- "There's something about gifts that seems odd. New abilities that are different than my natural ones? How does that relate to my real life and spiritual journey? Maybe that's why we moved on from talking about gifts."

What's interesting is that all these thoughts and feelings are reactions to a particular view on the topic of gifts. It's a view we assumed was the only view to have, so it became the popular view, even though it has its charismatic and noncharismatic variations. But there's another way to think about spiritual gifts, regardless of which variation of the popular view you side with.

In this book, you're going to hear about the Journey View—an alternative way to understand what spiritual gifts are about. My desire is to share with you how that understanding is both true to Scripture and relevant to our daily faith journey.

WHAT WE ARE GOING TO COVER

The popular view has been around for a while and has helped many people. It's made up of several beliefs about gifts that are shared by charismatics and noncharismatics alike, despite their well-known disagreements. The view you'll read here will be different than the popular emphases on gifts because:

- We won't focus on gifts as things we get. Instead, we will focus on people—who are filled with potential—all people.
- We'll learn how gift development is part of our journeys of growth—since our reality is that we're all in process as we try to live and serve others.
- We'll emphasize how our impact on one another matters much more than test results in helping us realize and live from our gifted potential.
- We'll get to these different perspectives mainly by exploring scriptural context and overlooked metaphors that are connected to spiritual gifts.

INTRODUCTION

As you read this book, you may think that I'm not sticking to the topic of spiritual gifts. That's because, as implied above, this view thoroughly integrates gifting with our journeys of growth and with loving community. I hope to show you the biblical rationale for that broader, true-to-life understanding of gifts.

Just as I will be sharing with you a view on gifts that includes ideas you haven't typically connected with the topic, *Spiritual Gifts Reimagined* will also leave out subjects you'd expect to find in a book on spiritual gifts.

For example, I won't be giving you my idea of the correct list of gifts with a definition of each. Why? I don't think that's where the emphasis is supposed to be.[1] We'll explore that. Also missing here are arguments on either side of the charismatic questions. To focus on that debate obscures our view, I believe, of the main scene of gifting—which we'll dive into here.

FRESH AND TIMELY

If you think it's time for a fresh approach to spiritual gifts, and if you are open to considering biblical threads that will broaden and deepen your perspective on gifts in Scripture and in life, please read on.

I'm humbled by the reality that many authors and teachers have preceded me in presenting their perspectives on gifts. I respect each one and am grateful for their contributions to the body of Christ. They have spread the truth that all of God's people are gifted for ministry.

I'm also humbled because I'm suggesting a view at odds with the widely accepted traditional beliefs about gifts. But I am encouraged by these words from evangelical scholar Dr. Grant Osborne in his book *The Hermeneutical Spiral*:

> The content of the doctrine (the extent to which it is based upon biblical teaching) is inviolate, but its expression or redescription changes as the thought processes of a culture change. Therefore, the way a systematic theology or individual doctrine will be expressed should alter from generation to generation and from culture to culture.[2]

After I wrote the final project for my Doctor of Ministry on this view of gifts in 1998, I continued to hear about our culture's transition from modern to postmodern thinking. Measured by Scripture, I think both philosophies fall short of a Christian worldview. But I started to perceive that the popular view of spiritual gifts, which I had come to see as mechanistic, was marked by modern thinking.

I also realized that the view of gifts I arrived at from studying Scripture emphasized metaphor and personal journey, two ideas related to postmodern thinking. It seems to me that this Journey View of gifts may be, to use Osborne's thought, a timely "redescription" of this doctrine that connects with the postmodern generation and culture.

This book, then, invites you to a reimagining of spiritual gifts that discovers their relevance in our life stories.

THIS BOOK'S ORGANIZATION

As already implied, the starting premise of this Journey View is that, when the Epistles present spiritual gifts to us, they are not listing abilities we get at some point. They are categorizing the diversity of people God has created and are pointing to an integration of gifts with growth. That premise will be explained and supported throughout this book.

In parts 1 and 2 we will first unpack many aspects of the life relevance of this view. Part 3 will then speak about strategies for applying the Journey View in and beyond church, and part 4 will contrast the Journey View with other views and study relevant biblical and conceptual perspectives.

The game plan of this book, then, is first to biblically explore the many facets of how the Journey View works out in our lives, leaving more detailed study of the undergirding scriptural interpretations for later. Here's a closer look at how the book develops:

Part 1 offers a panoramic overview of the high peaks of gifts reimagined. My goal in part 1 is to inspire you to perceive, through the window of spiritual gifts,

- the beauty of variegated humanity
- the journey of developing your unique potentials/gifts
- the wisdom of the cross needed to live with gifted diversity
- the love we journeyers need to receive and give

Yes, I believe that spiritual gifting is a window into these powerful realities. A Christian leader told me recently that he thought, after all the publications and presentations about gifts in the last several decades, Christians are bored with the subject. If that's true for you, I hope I can disrupt your boredom! One way Scripture disrupts our thinking is by throwing metaphors at us, suggesting wiser ways to perceive life.³ In part 1 we'll be diving into biblical metaphors related to gifting.

In part 2 you'll meet Jaden, whom I'd like to recruit into youth ministry. Chapters 5 through 8 break out the dimensions of his gifting journey and yours, shared from the perspective of a pastor. It details your practical process in growing as a person gifted by God.

At the end of each chapter in parts 1 and 2, you'll find reflection questions. They can be used individually or by a small group.

In part 3 we'll shift to strategic thinking about how the Journey View applies to life and ministry in the church, and to outreach into our world. We all expect that someone teaching a view of spiritual gifts will show us how it works in the church. But you'll see that the nature of the Journey View leads to a broader church application than you might expect.

What is not usually expected in a book about spiritual gifts is a chapter on why gifts are relevant for unbelievers, too, clarifying a fundamental area of common ground all humans share with one another. Chapter 11 explores how the Journey View of spiritual gifts positions Christians to witness Christ to a world passionate about embracing diversity and grappling with the quest to find each one's true self.

While parts 1 through 3 are application-oriented, they follow biblical threads related to spiritual gifts that broaden our thinking on this topic. Although part 4 focuses more intently on Scripture interpretation, you'll need the input of parts 1 through 3 to accompany the more detailed studies in part 4, where I shift to a more analytical approach.

INTRODUCTION

Part 4 presents three interpretive options for understanding gifts, gives clearer explanations of how and why I interpret and apply the relevant scriptures as I do, and covers additional related topics. It should help answer questions about why this approach is so different than the traditional teachings about gifts: why I emphasize certain ideas and deemphasize others.

Are you ready to reimagine spiritual gifts? You will need your imagination in this study. I don't say this because your imagination or mine should be our guide; Scripture is to be our guide. Yet in his wisdom, God delighted in sprinkling throughout Scripture a creative gallery of images.

They are meant to help us discover and grasp the realities we're invited to in knowing Christ and journeying with him. Spiritual gift truth in Scripture points to some of those inspiring images. You will need to use the tool of your imagination to perceive and apply them.

Please join me as we consider a familiar topic from a fresh perspective. Let's reimagine spiritual gifts!

PART ONE

TAKE IN THE PANORAMA

Popular books on spiritual gifts often feel like how-to manuals. We think what we've discovered in the New Testament is simply practical insight into how churches and individual Christians can function and serve more effectively. So we've lifted the verses on gifts out of the Bible and created our books, classes, and tests. Our focus is how to determine which added gifts you have and how to use them.

This how-to approach has helped many people become involved in ministry. But in our enthusiasm for applying these practical insights, we have typically not discerned how the theme of spiritual gifts is integrated with the rest of Scripture, nor how the gifts in each of us are integrated with our unique identities and journeys. Those ideas do not easily fit into a how-to manual.

In the biblical texts about gifts and their contexts, there are clues to what we have overlooked. Those clues point beyond the how-to template we have used and steer us toward a panoramic view of God's multifaceted wisdom displayed through spiritual gifts. These scriptural clues provoke our imaginations as they invite us into the adventure of growing with one another as the uniquely crafted creations of God we each are.

While there are biblical studies reflected in each of the next four chapters, each one can also be used as a meditation. If you engage with the teachings this way, these four themes will help prepare you for perceiving and applying the reimagined view of gifts presented here. Let's take in the panorama!

CHAPTER ONE

SPECTRUM OF GRACE

Spiritual gifts are an invitation to amazement and appreciation, to wonder at the vastly varied beauty of God's grace and wisdom seen through humanity.

Every time we rounded a bend in the road, we felt amazed. Huge rock formations, colorful and varied, filled one panorama after another. Miles of high desert beauty and mystery thrilled us as we crept along like ants on winding roads in a universe of splendor and grandeur.

Susan and I were celebrating our wedding anniversary amid the early fall foliage in western Colorado and the wide expanses of eastern Utah. We live in a beautiful area in Missouri, but our breath was taken away by the rugged wonders farther west in God's imaginative creation.

Beauty is *his* signature. And he knew we humans would be amazed and awed by the stunning masterpieces that flowed out of the heart of our world's Creator. Since God obviously values beauty, he himself must have first been thrilled, feeling deep joy as he imagined and crafted all that magnificence.

And what about us? Aren't we God's handiwork? As the days of creation unfolded throughout Genesis 1, his verdict was consistent: "God saw that it was good," and it rises in crescendo. It climaxed in his joyful and satisfied it is "very good!" on the day he created man and woman in his image.

We are expressions of his creativity and imagination—each a delight to him. So that encompasses the variety within our human race, doesn't it? Just as the many other facets of his creation are diverse, so are his human creations. In fact, the vast and endless variety in creation is one of the big reasons we are awed by it. Variety seems as much his signature as beauty.

PETER'S PICTURE

We begin our reimagining of spiritual gifts by pondering what God envisioned when he created the human race, which would include variety and beauty. Humanity created by God displays, through his eyes, delightful diversity. We are given a clue about the beauty of this variety in one of the four New Testament passages about spiritual gifts:

> As each has received a gift, use it to serve one another, as good stewards of God's varied grace: whoever speaks, as one who speaks oracles of God; whoever serves, as one who serves by the strength that God supplies—in order that in everything God may be glorified through Jesus Christ. To him belong glory and dominion forever and ever. Amen. (1 Peter 4:10-11)

We read in these two verses that each Christian is gifted by God, and we are called to use these gifts to serve one another. As we serve through our gifts, we're letting God touch others' lives through us. Peter says this brings glory to God through Jesus. What a wonderful plan in which God has given each of us the potential to impact one another in positive and constructive ways!

Yet there's more in these two verses than a plan; there's also a picture. There are more than written instructions here; there is a visual image. That image is not captured well by Bible translations. It is inserted by Peter when he describes God's grace in 4:10: Peter agrees with Paul that spiritual gifts are expressions of God's grace, and as he describes the grace of God seen through our gifts, he uses the Greek adjective *poikilos*.[1]

The most common English translation of *poikilos* in this verse is "manifold." Next is "varied." It was mostly used in the Greek spoken in that era to describe an artistic creation, usually visual. Its basic meaning is "many-colored" or "variegated." Writers used it to capture the beauty in works of fabric, metal, painting, architecture, or music. Sometimes it referred to intricacy and complexity.[2]

We were just thinking about variety and beauty, weren't we? It makes sense that the grace of God expressed through spiritual gifts displays variety. Peter finds *poikilos* a great way to imagine God's grace, and I think its basic meaning of variegated fits well. He is speaking about people who are gifted by God, and we are his artistic creations. We are his variegated grace, an art gallery full of grace-expressions.

Based on Peter's word *poikilos*, I prefer to exclaim his exhortation about our beautiful variety in 1 Peter 4:10 this way: "Be good stewards of God's spectrum of grace!"

This word picture of the grace expressed through such a vast and colorful variety of gifted people invites spontaneous wonder, amazement, and delight—just as Susan and I had our breath taken away by the landscapes of Colorado and Utah. Time and again, we exclaimed, "Wow!" Until the words "wow" and "amazing" seemed inadequate in the face of God's artistic creation.

To realize that God has created the variegated beauty that is us says a lot about him and us. He is proud of us. God considers us each a worthy expression of himself. He delights in the gifted uniqueness of each of us. He is imaginative in his design of each one. And, as Peter wrote, he is glorified when we express our gifted diversity.

We are his spectrum of grace. It is grace that makes that variegated display beautiful. For we are beautiful to him not only because of his creation of us, but also due to his re-creation of us through salvation in Jesus. Grace brings us the deliverance we need. Then we can step into the development of our giftedness that more and more displays his artistry through each of us. We'll talk more about that development of giftedness in later chapters.

He made us each to be our own hue on that spectrum of grace—your unique hue. How many hues or colors do you think there are on God's spectrum of grace? In physics we learn that a true spectrum of colors varies smoothly and gradually all along the spectrum. They say that we see such a spectrum when we see white light split by a prism.

A rainbow reminds us of it, though it's composed of only a handful of mixed colors, not a pure spectrum. But because of a pure spectrum's smooth variation from one hue to the next to the next, there are an infinite number of distinct spectral colors.[3] An infinite number of distinct colors—now that's an interesting illustration. It takes myriads of unique, grace-transforming people to express the creative wonder of God!

It's interesting because Peter's list of gifts is the shortest in the New Testament—two gifts: serving and speaking. You can count those on one hand. But all the toes and fingers of you and all your friends aren't enough to tally the number of different grace hues we are on God's spectrum. What does that suggest to us about Peter's list of gifts? The same is true of Paul's lists. We'll be delving into that in later chapters. Speaking of Paul . . .

PAUL'S BREATH IS TAKEN AWAY

While there may be an infinite number of colors in the spectrum of a prism, certainly God knows the exact number of people he creates and re-creates. But it's a big number! In fact, the apostle Paul felt the word *poikilos* wasn't vast enough, so when he reached for it to describe another characteristic of God displayed through God's people (Ephesians 3:10), he tacked a preposition on the front of it: *polu-poikilos! God's super-variegated wisdom!*[4]

If you listen for Paul's heartbeat as you read Ephesians, you will realize that he is passionate—full of wonder—about "the mystery," once hidden but now unveiled. The mystery is that God is creating one body of people—a united body saved by the grace flowing to us through Jesus. In Ephesians 3, his passion escalates from verse to verse:

- "The mystery was made known to me by revelation" (3:3).
- The mystery "was not made known to the sons of men in other generations as it has now been revealed" (3:5).

- "Gentiles are fellow heirs, members of the same body, and partakers of the promise in Christ Jesus through the gospel" (3:6).
- "Though I am the very least of all the saints, this grace was given, to preach to the Gentiles the unsearchable riches of Christ" (3:8).
- It is time "to bring to light for everyone what is the plan of the mystery hidden for ages" (3:9).

These verses were written, and are meant to be read, with an intensifying crescendo of enthusiasm. Allow me to paraphrase Paul's eruption of wonder at the climax of this crescendo:

> This was all so that the super-variegated wisdom of God would now be made known, through the church, to the rulers and authorities in heavenly realms! And this lines up with God's eternal purpose, which is now coming to fruition in Christ Jesus our Lord! (Ephesians 3:10–11)

Wow! Paul is like a man crawling up the side of a mountain, reaching the peak, standing up to see the panorama, and then, in amazement, almost falling over at the sight! The mystery at long-last unveiled: God is creating a super-variegated body of people. It's not a monochrome, one-size-fits-all bunch. Why? Because he is so wise, Paul stated. In our diversity as his people, we display not only God's spectrum of grace but also his spectrum of wisdom.

While the uniting of diverse races into one body (Jew and Gentile in Ephesians 2) is the lead-up to Paul's enthusiastic words, this wisdom of God flows into our unity amid spiritual gift diversity

(Ephesians 4). We'll be looking at some of that later, connecting Paul's metaphor of the body of Christ with his guidance about gifts.

But as we contemplate the vast and variegated grace and wisdom of God displayed through his people, let's consider how much we need to allow those truths to penetrate our hearts.

THE PRISM OF GRACE

We've begun our reimagining of spiritual gifts by focusing on this beautiful spectrum because I can't even count how many times I have stumbled over that variety as I've encountered this expression and that expression of God's grace that is different than me! Since I'm one of billions, I'm constantly encountering different people—even those who are like me are *not exactly* like me!

I served as a pastor for twenty years, and that's a role that surely requires a person to see, value, and embrace God's spectrum of grace in a congregation. But I'd say I sometimes missed that wisdom because of focusing on my own wisdom. His wisdom is bigger. It is broader. It is breathtaking, leaving us in wonder.

I think I did better at seeing his wisdom when I later served as a chaplain and intensive workshop leader, focusing on one person at a time, or on small groups of people. Listening, learning, marveling, and encouraging each person to discover who they are on God's spectrum of grace and wisdom. You see, growing into the authentic and unique *you* is one of the ways you fulfill Peter's admonition to be a "good steward" of God's spectrum. We'll also talk more about that later.

This is where the illustration of a prism helps me. I'm sure Peter and Paul were smart guys, but they weren't physicists and probably didn't study about prisms refracting light into an infinite spectrum. Yet the metaphor of grace as a prism reminds me that all these diverse people I don't understand are refracted, unique masterpieces of God's grace. And yes, they're in process. But aren't we all?

And wouldn't you say that "serving one another as good stewards of God's spectrum of grace" implies an environment of grace in which we appreciate one another? If Paul and Peter celebrated the variegated beauty they saw in the church, then I need to ask myself if my heart participates in that celebration. Later, we'll talk more about the importance of grace and love in our development as uniquely gifted people.

CLOSING THOUGHTS

I'd like to conclude this opening chapter with a couple of thoughts. First, presentations about spiritual gifts often have a utilitarian feel. We tend to emphasize that gifts are about what we do (tasks), not so much about who we are (being). This book takes a different approach. What we do is important, but it flows out of who we are.

I haven't yet laid out my case to you that spiritual gifts are broader than just certain abilities we receive from God. But I've highlighted for you that *poikilos* is a clue, through the two apostles who wrote about gifts, that their significance is greater than merely the tasks we do.

We are invited to see beauty and to respond with wonder. We are asked to imagine each person as a grace-expression. We are to be amazed at all this as a key unveiling of God's wisdom. And we are to approach Peter and Paul's direct teachings about gifts with the awareness that finite lists of gifts are a tool they employed to talk about a magnificent and myriad reality. It's beyond tasks and abilities; it's about you, me, and us.

Second, we've explored the reality that the display of God's grace and wisdom through the gifted uniqueness of each of us is marked by diversity. Currently, our society talks a lot about diversity, advancing its own definitions and guidance about it.

As we navigate through our world's ideas about diversity, it's easy to forget about the godly diversity referred to in Scripture, which our variegated spiritual gifts display. The human diversity God has created is shaped by his grace and wisdom, not by what the society of today or tomorrow says. We need a godly vision of human diversity, and that can only come through knowing deeply the One who imagined and created the spectrum of his grace that we are.

In chapter 11 we'll consider further how we, as hues on God's spectrum of grace, relate to unbelievers looking for their identities. And we'll touch on how the Journey View of spiritual gifts has something to say to a society defining diversity and identity differently than God does in his Word.

You may be thinking that this chapter is an odd way to begin a study on spiritual gifts. The popular view has conditioned us to expect that we'll focus on gift lists, definitions, and uses. Instead, I've asked you to use your imagination around one overlooked word—*poikilos*. Imagining God's spectrum of grace can be a first step into seeing spiritual gifts differently. Chapter 2 will be a second step in that direction.

FOR REFLECTION AND LISTENING

> *The spiritual director is in an enviable place to observe the endless variations of grace, the fantastic fertility of the divine Spirit bringing faith into creation.*
>
> —EUGENE PETERSON[5]

1. Why are wonder and beauty important as I respond to all the gifted diversity around me?

2. How can I grow in my appreciation of God's spectrum of grace and wisdom that is displayed by the variety of people around me? In my home, my church, and my world?

3. Is the "enviable place" Peterson talks about exclusive to spiritual directors? What would it be like to have eyes that enjoy and glorify God for "the endless variations of grace"?

CHAPTER TWO

THE SPOILS JOURNEY

There is a historical precedent to spiritual gifts, and it illustrates gifting as a journey. Imagining ourselves on that journey opens the path to enrichment with our gifts as we grow. Our part is to engage with the battles on that journey.

We are inspired by stories of courage—stories that depict people facing obstacles of many kinds. They capture our imaginations with the battles courageous people have fought. Think William Wallace in Scotland, Harriet Tubman in America, Anne Frank in the Netherlands, or Nelson Mandela in South Africa.

These epic sagas are full of drama, suspense, formidable enemies, doubt, fear, intrigue, faith, and vision. They have spawned novels and movies, and through them we find ourselves encouraged in our own journeys. After all, obstacles and battles are a part of every human life.

What does this have to do with spiritual gifts? Provocatively, the apostle Paul began his Ephesians discussion of spiritual gifts by teasing our imaginations:

But to each one of us grace has been given as Christ apportioned it. This is why it says: "When he ascended on high, he led captives in his train and gave gifts to men." (What does "he ascended" mean except that he also descended to the lower, earthly regions? He who descended is the very one who ascended higher than all the heavens, in order to fill the whole universe.) (Ephesians 4:7–10 NIV)

Verses 8–10 are not what we expect to find in teachings about gifts! When we turn to the scriptures about gifts, we expect to find pragmatic guidance about Christians usefully serving one another in personal and church ministries. But here in Ephesians, Paul immediately began his workshop on gifts by painting a picture!

He wants me to imagine Christ ascending and leading captives in his train. We're looking for hands-on, user-friendly instructions, and here we get some mysterious, symbolic imagery that apparently involves prisoners of war (not to mention descending and ascending how many times?). And the apostle wants us to believe it's important in order to understand spiritual gifts.

GIFTING HAS BEEN SEEN BEFORE

Paul is pointing us to a story. He actually points us to a metanarrative (a big, overarching story) containing many stories—numerous epic sagas of courage and fear, victory and loss. And he says that gifting was seen before in those stories. Paul wants us to understand spiritual gifts through the grid of a big story. His words in Ephesians 4:8 serve as a kind of hyperlink to Psalm 68:18 where we read, "You ascended on high, leading a host of captives in your train and receiving gifts among men."

In that Old Testament verse, we see God as King ascending to his throne, vanquished captives following him. We can see that Paul draws a parallel between the ascent of Christ and this ascent of God in Psalm 68. But we're left with questions: Why does Paul bring up Christ's ascent in a discussion of gifts? How is the ascent in Psalm 68 relevant? And—I'm guessing you noticed this—how can Paul just change the idea of *God receiving gifts* to *Christ giving gifts* when he cites this psalm?

We're going to answer those questions and learn why Psalm 68 is relevant for understanding spiritual gifting. Let's first get an overview of the Psalm 68 background story Paul brings to our attention.

Some scholars believe this psalm written by King David was perhaps composed for the celebration when Israel's ark of the covenant was brought to Jerusalem and carried up into the Holy of Holies on Mount Zion (2 Samuel 6).[1] It is poetic, as are all psalms. As the title of Psalm 68 indicates, these lyrics were given to the choir director, and the words were heartily and beautifully sung in celebration of this climactic occasion.

Psalm 68 remembers God delivering Israel from one foe after another. There are hints of their powerful exodus from Egypt.[2] This song also reminded them that God faithfully fought for them as they journeyed to and into the land promised to them, conquering that territory one battle at a time. The battle most clearly alluded to in 68:8–9 is Deborah's victory over Sisera in Judges 4–5.[3]

Israel regarded the ark of the covenant as God's throne.[4] They must have felt great exhilaration, because now, at last, God their victorious Warrior King is ascending to his throne (68:17–18). I say "at last" because this festive and joyful inauguration fulfilled centuries-old promises and followed centuries of dramatic stories of courage, battles, *and gifting.*

Wow! We're far afield from a study of spiritual gifts, aren't we? Egypt, the ark, Deborah? Let's take stock of where we are. In Ephesians 4:8, Paul zeroed in on a victorious ascent, vanquished foes, and gifts. David focused on those also in Psalm 68:18. But what we learn in the psalm is that the gifts are spoils of battles—spoils that ended up enriching God's people.

> "Kings and armies flee, they flee, and she who remains at home will divide the spoil!" When you lie down among the sheepfolds, you are like the wings of a dove covered with silver, and its pinions with glistening gold. (Psalm 68:12–13 NASB)

God's people end up enriched—like a glistening dove—with the spoils of victorious battles. These spoils, first received by their Warrior King (68:18), were then distributed to them. God removed from enemy control the riches he intended for his people. *I believe Paul wants us to see spiritual gifts as riches our victorious ascending Christ takes from enemy control. Those gifts flow through his hands as he gives them to us, so they are both received by the King and given to his people.*[5]

In other words, according to Paul, gifting has been seen before. We've just looked at the part of this background that focuses us on our victorious King. We now turn our attention to the part of this gifting background that focuses on our role: engagement with the battles.

BATTLES ON THE JOURNEY

Are you beginning to reimagine spiritual gifts? This historical precedent suggests that they are won at great cost; enemies have to be faced; and gifts are the spoils of actual battles. You see, the poetic jubilation of Psalm 68 reflects real history: stories recorded in the books of Exodus, Numbers, Joshua, Judges, Samuel, and so on.

In those often-neglected pages, we see battle after battle against enemy after enemy. And the spoils won in every victorious battle were God's gifts to his people, according to Psalm 68. Obviously, God's people were not passive observers in those battles!

In fact, as we look at the sweep of Old Testament history Psalm 68 points to, we see that God's agenda for his people involved one battle after another. That's not because God likes battles. It's because God loves to gift his people. Why does that involve battles? It's because the gifts happen to be in enemy hands!

Think about it. God promised Abraham, Isaac, and Jacob that he would take the land of Canaan out of enemy hands and gift it to their descendants (Genesis 15:18–21; 26:3–4; 28:13; 35:12). When the process began to get underway, he told Moses he'd deliver Israel from Egypt, so effectively that they would carry out the Egyptians' riches (spoils) with them, which is just what happened (Exodus 3:20–22; 12:35-36; cf. Genesis 15:13–14).

Then on the way to and in the promised land, God challenged his people to face, battle, conquer, and plunder enemy after enemy. The result would be, the Lord said, that he would gift them with

> Great and splendid cities which you did not build, and houses full of all good things which you did not fill, and hewn cisterns which you did not dig, vineyards and olive trees which you did not plant, and you [shall] eat and [be] satisfied. (Deuteronomy 6:10–11 NASB)

It seems like it's God's standard operating procedure to transfer riches to his people—riches that have been in enemy hands but which he intends for his people to have. It also seems to be his normal plan to expect our participation in the process—following him into the battles.

We could've started our study of Paul's teaching about gifts in Ephesians by reading 4:7 and then jumping to 4:11–16. That way, we could stick with the more familiar and seemingly more usable information about how the church works. The ideas in those verses are very important. But Paul doesn't want us to detour around 4:8–10.[6] He guides us into this big story about spoils. Why? As one Bible scholar puts it, Paul believed the Old Testament "creates understanding" for us.[7]

Ephesians 4:8 is like the wardrobe in The Chronicles of Narnia.[8] Following Paul through the back of the wardrobe, we are led into a panoramic story of how God enriches his people with gifts. Our understanding is enlarged. We are invited to use our imaginations to see our own lives as a journey into the riches God has designed for us, and the battles to retrieve those riches.

This backstory is out of sync with the popular thinking that spiritual gifts are automatically added new abilities. I don't think Paul understood gifts that way. I think he saw them as the fruits of victories we need to experience along our journeys as we follow our Warrior Christ.[9]

THE SPOILS JOURNEY

Your potentials await your growth. The specific and unique ways you can impact others depend on your own progress as you mature in your journey. The availability of your spiritual gifts for your use depends on you facing and following God into the battles he knows you must fight in order to heal and grow. All of this is because your potentials are held hostage by the enemy—by sin and immaturity. God intends for you to plunder those enemies, retrieving the awesome potentials he created in you.

This calls for courage. You will need courage to fight your battles. It is courage based on confidence in God your Warrior, who promises victory. Paul, in mentioning Christ's victorious ascent (4:8) is telling us that the biggest battle has already been fought and won by Christ. But our journeys of battles are still there. They wait for you to engage and fight, trusting him.

There are many battle stories in the Old Testament, and many scenes of God enriching his people with spoils through those battles. Yet God's people were not always faithful to follow him into the battles, sometimes running away in fear. The most famous of those stories played out at Kadesh Barnea.

God brought them to the border of the promised land and challenged them to engage in the battles to take it. He promised he would be with them and give them victory. But when their advance spies reported there were giants in the land, they cowered in fear and refused to face into the necessary battles. As a result, the rich gifts God intended to bestow on them were postponed. They wandered in the wilderness for forty years (Numbers 13–14).

YOUR BATTLEGROUNDS

Receiving your gifts from God is not a passive affair.[10] They are spoils of the battles you must fight in your growth journey. *No battles, no spoils.* The Old Testament battlegrounds were each successive region of Canaan. The plan was for them to progressively retrieve each piece of turf, taking it out of enemy hands.

Where are our battlegrounds today? The scriptures of the Old and New Testaments make it clear that our hearts are the scenes of struggle. Our hearts may be divided. Or they may be following the Lord, or running from him. Sometimes they're back and forth, much like a pinball machine.

I have fought some of the battles God wants me to fight, so I've discovered and developed some of the gifts he has given to me, which I've used to serve others. But there are also battles I've avoided. So those spoils are postponed, in limbo. That means that my potentials to impact others in even more ways are stunted. There is still turf in my heart that sits in enemy hands. Those battles await my courage and my confidence in God—my Warrior King.

Spiritual gifts are the riches or powers God creates in people, which were wrongly taken by God's enemies but are now retrieved by him as he marches to victory. They are the potentials and abilities God wired into us when he created each one of us. Sin claimed these potentials—our own sins and the effects of others' sins against us.

God's deliverance (salvation) begins a process of retrieving those lost and buried riches. He progressively restores those potentials if we consistently follow him through the battles of our Christian journeys. So spiritual gifts are our God-given potentials that have been lost to sin. But they are now the spoils of battles in which God leads us in victory after victory.

COUNTING ON RESTORATION

Perhaps this raises a question in your mind. I don't know about you, but if I were to chart my spiritual growth on a graph, you would not see a smooth line consistently trending upward. It might look more like the horizon of a mountain range! If discovery and use of my gifts depends on my growth, I may be in trouble. My gifts may remain dormant for a long time; or my motives, focus, and wisdom while using my gifts might be very inconsistent.

The damages of sin within us are real, obstructing the gifting process. The discovery, development, and use of our spiritual gifts awaits our spiritual growth. So if your growth is stalled out—if your faithfulness to follow God into the necessary battles is inconsistent—what hope is there for you to live and serve in the grace and power of the gifts he has put within you?

Remember, as Paul indicated in Ephesians 4:8, gifting has been seen before. He pointed us to the gifting journey of Israel. Sometimes they faithfully followed him into battles and reaped the rich spoils that came with the victories, removing from enemy hands the wealth God intended for them.

But as I already mentioned, they were extremely inconsistent and did not remain faithful to God and his vision for them. Eventually they found themselves in captivity to their oppressors. That's when God made his promise of *restoration* loud and clear—a promise that reaffirms his earlier promises that they would be enriched with the spoils of their battles for their promised land.

His promise to them, after grieving and disciplining them for their failures, was: "I will restore your fortunes!" The phrase rings in our ears around seventeen times in Old Testament prophecy. Our failures and inconsistencies are parts of all our stories. But all our stories are ultimately about our gracious, restoring God. Hope for each of us comes from God's response to our inconsistencies and our ongoing failures in grace: "I [will] restore your fortunes before your very eyes" (Zephaniah 3:20 NIV).

If you start out on the journey of reclaiming your gifted potentials that have been damaged and buried, but then slide back, like God's people at Kadesh Barnea and many other times, God promises to restore you. He promises to never let go of his vision of you as enriched with all the spoils he's allotted to you.

You can count on God's restoring grace!

CLOSING THOUGHTS

We've covered a lot in this chapter. If you want to do a deeper dive into the fifty-plus times the theme of spoils comes up in the Old Testament and the seventeen times God promises to restore his people's fortunes, check out appendix 2 at the end of the book. Also, in part 4 I will present my arguments in greater detail for this view of gifts as spoils.

There's more to say about God's vision of you as enriched by his gifts for you, and we'll look at that in chapter 5. There's also more to say about the battles involved on our gifting journeys. We'll look at that more closely in chapter 6.

Before I opened up this imaginative wardrobe and stumbled into this journey understanding of gifting and spoils, I believed God zapped me with some spiritual gifts when I got saved. I felt they were different than my natural abilities, and that I could take some tests and learn what those gifts were. Then I was responsible to find ministry roles that matched my gifts.

But now I find myself inspired by the big story. It's an epic saga of my King, who leads his people, powerfully helps me tackle the enemies within me, and richly restores within my heart my true identity and potentials so that I am someone whose life today has impact and meaning.

Out of all that, I can powerfully serve people in ministries. I know that's an ideal, and I know I'm just as prone to fear and retreat as God's people of old. But I'm inspired. My imagination is enlivened and my courage elevated. Hope is revived. Adventures await. I'm part of a story bigger than me.

FOR REFLECTION AND LISTENING

The Bible assumes that its stories are also our story.

—DAN ALLENDER[11]

1. How have you seen your personal growth (and others' personal growth) lead to discovery, development, and use of your (and their) gifted potentials?

2. Their story is your story; their journey yours. Thinking of Allender's statement about the Bible's stories, what feelings arise in you when you imagine yourself as invited by God to retrieve your spoils/gifts that are in enemy hands?

3. The ascended Christ has won your victory. But what battles are awaiting your engagement, requiring your faith and courage?

CHAPTER THREE

CROSS WISDOM

We stumble over the beautiful diversity of spiritual gifts through our judgments about others and ourselves. The wisdom of the cross transforms us into a gathering of the humble and honoring, in which every part of Christ's body is valued.

The professor stood in the hall outside the room where his class had just dismissed. I didn't know it—but he was waiting for me. As a seminary student in my mid-twenties, one of my various immaturities was arrogance. Like most people who are arrogant, I was insensitive to the ways it bled through in my words and actions.

I don't remember my teacher's exact words to me. But humbly and respectfully he asked if he had offended me. Based on my questions in class, he sensed my attitude toward him was negative. His words lovingly slammed me right between the eyes with hard truth. I was judging my brother in Christ and his teaching gift. Thinking I was wiser than my professor, the words and tone in my questions betrayed sarcasm toward, and feelings of superiority over, this godly man.

My professor and I seemed to have very different personalities. Also, though I ended up using the gift of teaching in my own career, our styles were quite dissimilar. When we encounter people who are not like ourselves, we are tempted to judge. Even if we are both serving God but doing it differently, we assess our way of serving as better than another's.

In chapter 1 we imagined the beauty and wisdom of God's spectrum of grace. His people are that spectrum, and God intends that we be awed and inspired by it—by every amazing hue on his spectrum. It is an ideal picture of gifted diversity.

But you and I are not ideal. As flawed sinners, we make judgments about some of the hues of grace on God's spectrum. Sometimes we're devaluing hues different than our own. Other times we're judging our own hue as less valuable than others. Now and then we're on the receiving end: judged by others as less than important.

We stumble over God's wisdom of gifted diversity—in friendships, family, small groups, or our workplaces—and the church has not been immune from this. The problem started in the first century, so we have in the New Testament an apostle's letter to a church struggling with God's spectrum of grace. In this letter, 1 Corinthians, we learn that a certain kind of wisdom—cross wisdom—is crucial as a foundation for our experience of gifted diversity.

GIFTED DIVERSITY REQUIRES WISDOM

Paul presents this foundational wisdom in 1 Corinthians 1. But before we look at that, we note that in his primary chapter on spiritual gifts in this letter, 1 Corinthians 12, he presents the wisdom of the body metaphor. He asks us to imagine the church as a human body in which every member is important. Using this lens is an important step in seeing one another as God sees us: "For the body does not consist of one member but of many" (12:14). "Now you are the body of Christ and individually members of it" (12:27).

As Paul describes the dynamics of each body part depending on all the other parts, he challenges us to stop acting like we don't need every other grace-expression (the plural Greek term is *charismata*) in Christ's body (see 12:12–27). The tone of Paul's instruction here is to correct: stop behaving like some gift expressions are more needed than others; live interdependently with one another, realizing that you need every other body member.[1]

That body wisdom, however, is based in a deeper truth found in 1 Corinthians 1.[2] It is a truth that levels the playing field. It exposes that our default attitudes, which may elevate some gift expressions and diminish others, are at odds with a reality at the core of Christian faith: the cross of Christ.

In 1 Corinthians 1:10–31, Paul exhorts us to not be fixated on gifted human influencers, but instead to be humbled by the cross of Christ. Within the church, we often find ourselves impressed if we perceive another Christian seems powerful and wise—or if we see ourselves that way. Paul's concern is that a focus on gifts of power and wisdom diminishes our focus on the cross of Christ.

> For Jews demand signs and Greeks seek wisdom, but we preach Christ crucified, a stumbling block to Jews and folly to Gentiles, but to those who are called, both Jews and Greeks, Christ the power of God and the wisdom of God. For the foolishness of God is wiser than men, and the weakness of God is stronger than men. (1:22–25)

According to Paul, the cross appears to be an image of weakness and foolishness, and he wants us to be humbled by that. It would be wise for each of us to stop right now and meditate on that. If I identify myself with the crucified Jesus, I am saved by the power and wisdom of God—cloaked in weakness and foolishness—whether I'm a famous and eloquent speaker or an unknown believer helping a homeless person. God did not choose any of us to be in Christ because he was impressed with us (1:26–31).

The wisdom of the cross, then, is that we are to be a gathering of the humble. We are not to be enamored with some gifted personalities, as the Corinthians were (1 Corinthians 1:10–13; 3:1–9). In tandem with the wisdom of the body, in which we honor every member as being strategic, *the wisdom we need to live in unity with our diverse spiritual gifts is to be a gathering of the humble and mutually honoring. That is cross wisdom.*

Therefore, in the diversified body of Christ, we each must choose between the wisdom of the cross and the wisdom of this world. The wisdom of this world leads to a prideful attitude about myself (such as my attitude toward my professor) or boastful identification with a leader I think is superior to others. (I've done that too!)

If we will elevate the ground-leveling wisdom of the cross to be our focus, we will see one another as grace-expressions (*charismata*). In humility, we will honor each person, including ourselves, as an amazing hue on God's spectrum of grace. I hope you can see why cross wisdom is an essential foundation—an essential spirituality—for living amidst gifted diversity.[3]

I call it a spirituality because it requires the work of God's Spirit in my spirit. I must journey from arrogance toward grace, from me-focus to we-focus. It takes all of us to manifest God's spectrum of grace and wisdom.

The pride of worldly wisdom, when it infects the church, blurs the beauty of the human spectrum God created to display his variegated wisdom through spiritual gifts. It is cross wisdom—in our hearts—that deflates that pride and unveils the beauty of the spectrum.

CROSS WISDOM ADDRESSES THREE PROBLEMS

Looking at 1 Corinthians 1, 3, and 12, we can conclude that cross wisdom—in tandem with body wisdom—will effectively undo three problems that can occur in human groups of any kind, including churches. Each of these problems will show up in our actions and words, but each begins in the attitudes of our hearts and the ideas in our heads—attitudes and ideas out of sync with cross wisdom.

Stratification

At times, we subconsciously have in our minds a hierarchy in which some people are more important than others. We create levels of value. This is not about whether some people, in using their gifts, have impact on greater numbers of people than others do. Of course that is the case. But are we confusing quantity with quality?

Are well-known Christian leaders of more value on God's spectrum of grace than those who are unknown? In my church, is the pastor of greatest value, the important teachers next in quality, then the heads of ministries, and finally, the gray mass of the rest who are like worker ants scurrying around?

Paul has a reminder for us if we are, even subconsciously, viewing God's people through a stratified grid that assigns high value to some gifts and low value to others. Besides the body teaching about needing every member, Paul bluntly stated:

> For consider your calling, brothers: not many of you were wise according to worldly standards, not many were powerful, not many were of noble birth. But God chose what is foolish in the world to shame the wise; God chose what is weak in the world to shame the strong; God chose what is low and despised in the world, even things that are not, to bring to nothing things that are, so that no human being might boast in the presence of God. (1 Corinthians 1:26–29)

A boastful attitude forgets that our status in God's sight, before and after salvation, is not one of being the cream of the crop. But a Christian with such a boastful attitude will stratify, from high to low, the value of gifted persons in the body of Christ. In this scenario, the diverse human spectrum God created is no longer based in grace, and its wisdom is not of the cross.

Paul wrote to the Corinthians that, within his own ministry among them and using his gifts, he sought to not be impressive but to lift up the cross (1 Corinthians 2:1–5). The gifted believer presenting Jesus to three kindergartners is as valuable as the gifted pastor preaching Jesus to three thousand. Only if I embrace the wisdom of the cross is that exciting to me.

Separation

The Corinthian church experienced lots of division (1:10–13), and the image of the body was intended to call them to unity

(1 Corinthians 12). In other words, to build unity in churches, Paul taught believers they are interconnected with one another as one organism. That goes deeper than the unity that organizations try to achieve. At the top of a good organization are leaders who proclaim their vision and values, and unity is achieved when employees operate according to those.

That approach is normal for an organization headed by humans. But Paul implies that the body of Christ internally relates differently. In the body metaphor, Christ is our head, and we are organically related, with both Christ and one another. In our organic oneness, we share the life flowing from the cross of Christ to every part of his body. Out of that new life we submit to Christ our head. This goes beyond organizational unity.

My experience is that often factions develop among God's people when we forget our identity as an organism and stop seeing one another as necessary contributing members in that organism. We begin to think and act like an organization.

Now organization is a necessary and useful tool, but in the body of Christ it should not compromise our identity as an organism.[4] The fact that we are brothers and sisters in Christ should season organizational realities with love and respect. The power and wisdom of the cross creates the living reality of us collectively being Christ's body in which the same life of Jesus flows through each of us (1 Corinthians 1:30) and connects us in him with one another.

This dynamic is behind Paul's presentations about spiritual gifts. His heart is to help us see our unity in our diversity and our diversity in our unity. Disagreements and offenses are to be expected in relationships, but when they happen, I have choices.

Will I emphasize where we agree or where we disagree? Will I keep in view that my brother or sister in Christ is a gifted expression of God on his spectrum of grace? Or will I focus on the ways I think they're wrong? Will I prioritize our organic connection through Jesus? Or will I shift to an organizational template, using its power to get my way? Cross wisdom keeps me focused on our organic unity in Christ.

Imitation

When we imitate others, we throw a monkey wrench into the spectrum of God's wisdom in which we're each to be our own unique and gifted color. I'm not talking about healthy imitation where I am inspired to be mature and godly like someone who is ahead of me on the path of growth. Paul implies there is an unhealthy imitation that is at odds with living as the body of Christ and with cross wisdom.

> If the foot should say, "Because I am not a hand, I do not belong to the body," that would not make it any less a part of the body. And if the ear should say, "Because I am not an eye, I do not belong to the body," that would not make it any less a part of the body. If the whole body were an eye, where would be the sense of hearing? If the whole body were an ear, where would be the sense of smell? (1 Corinthians 12:15–17)

The problematic attitude is "because I am not."

Link that with the Corinthians being enamored with certain gifted personalities (1:10–13; 3:1–9). If I am counting myself as having less value than someone else ("I'm just a foot, not a hand."),

and I'm really impressed with you and your gifts, I'll probably try to imitate you—even if I do so unconsciously. There are some churches, and other human groups, where this becomes the culture. The Corinthian church probably had a culture of imitation.

What is the motivation for imitation? "Because I am not a hand, I do not belong to the body." The motivation is to belong: desire for acceptance and fear of non-acceptance. When I see others accepted and celebrated, I think the ways they attained that status are the ways I need to attain it. In my pursuit of that acceptance, my uniqueness is suffocated, which results in the brilliance of God's spectrum of grace being dulled.

If I make the wisdom of the body metaphor my own, I will assert that, as a foot, I am not "any less a part of the body" than a hand. In Christ, each one of us represents a greater wisdom, power, and nobility than all the impressive people of the world (1:26–29), whether we're hands or feet or eyebrows or knees in the body of Christ!

And as we link 1 Corinthians 12 back to 1 Corinthians 1, that body wisdom is based on deeper cross wisdom—the wisdom of "Christ crucified" (1:23). You see, Jesus refused to imitate. He refused to try to impress. He did not need to pursue acceptance. We'll be further looking at how he lived according to cross wisdom in chapter 7 and examine why this is important as we reimagine spiritual gifts.

EACH OF US BEING OURSELVES

We've seen that cross wisdom leads us to embrace our gifted diversity within our organic unity, and that one application of this is that I am not to imitate others. God did not create me to look like you. If your character is more godly than mine, following the example of your godly character would be a good idea. But I am uniquely crafted to be a hue like no other on God's spectrum of grace.

Earlier, we noted that the body of Christ is to be a gathering of those who are humble and mutually honoring. I am to honor how you uniquely display God and his grace. You are to do the same for me. But do you and I honor ourselves in that way? Or do we devalue our own uniqueness, perhaps imitating others to gain acceptance?

Who you authentically are is acceptable in the body of Christ. Not only that, who you authentically are is needed and wanted in the body of Christ. In the world's thinking, you need to imitate to be accepted. In the body of Christ, we need the authentic you.[5]

In Christ, and in the body of Christ, you actually have a responsibility to be who you authentically are. The display of God's spectrum of grace, and the functioning of Christ's body, depends on each of us being ourselves. Years ago, a member of a church I served gave me a T-shirt that echoed this truth I had taught there. Across the front of the shirt it read: "Always being Bill is an awesome responsibility."

It's awesome because it's based in body wisdom, which is based in cross wisdom, which is all about Christ. In the gathering of those humbled by the cross, I honor your awesome responsibility to be you and my own to be mine. This is foundational to our engagement with the beauty and power of spiritual gifts. As we reimagine gifts, we must understand that our attitudes of arrogance and pride, our default tendencies to imitate impressive others, and our fears of not being accepted all gum up the works.

God calls his people to be a gathering of those who are humble and honoring.

Humbly, I acknowledge that I am not impressive in this world. Or that if I sometimes am, it has nothing to do with my true value. Humbly, I acknowledge that I am but one part of the body, needing all the other parts. Humbly, I receive honor from others who affirm that I am an amazing hue on God's spectrum, which is all due to grace. And joyfully, I honor others as equally amazing hues on God's spectrum of grace.

CLOSING THOUGHTS

Scripturally understood, the cross always challenges us. In this chapter we've seen one way its challenge cuts right into our hearts, where we have attitudes that cause us to stumble over the beautiful diversity of spiritual gifts. Those attitudes need to be replaced by cross wisdom.

We've wondered at God's spectrum of grace, discovered our spoils journeys, and are now tuning into the wisdom of the cross. These are three high peaks in the beautiful panorama of spiritual gifts. There is one more to consider before we dive deeper in part 2 into how we walk this journey. In chapter 4 we'll ponder our need for powerful love from one another in the gifting journey.

FOR REFLECTION AND LISTENING

The load, or weight, or burden of my neighbour's glory should be laid on my back, a load so heavy that only humility can carry it, and the backs of the proud will be broken.

—C. S. LEWIS[6]

1. Describe the spirit and environment you think would be experienced in a church that is a gathering of the humble and mutually honoring.

2. Where are you in your process of learning the wisdom of the cross and affirming the strategic importance of the gifts of those around you?

3. Ponder Lewis's words. What is your neighbor's glory? And what would it look like for you to receive the weight of your neighbor's glory laid daily on your back?

CHAPTER FOUR

POWERFUL LOVE

In our growth and gift development, we need one another. That need is at a deeper than superficial level and requires each of us to learn how to practice the biblical specifics of loving well.

Tom, Greg, and I usually met in a room about the size of a nice walk-in closet, sandwiched between the sanctuary and church lobby. Our weekly connection was about just that—connecting. The group had shrunk from five or six men to three, in part because we decided to make it about sharing our journeys instead of going through a discipleship study book.

I look back on the years I spent with my two friends as some of the most important in my growth journey. The reason is that the dynamic of truth working in love permeated our interactions. We each brought the real stuff of our lives and laid it out for examination. We allowed one another to see the good and not-so-good of our lives, and we developed an enthusiasm for each other.

The truth revealed about me to my friends was both my corruption and my glory, my failures and my potentials (gifts). Their love responded through their belief in me, their treasuring of me, and their excitement when I moved even a little toward the glory of who God made me to be. Jesus "shows up," in love, when we start dealing with the truth about him and about ourselves. That is when powerful relating begins too.[1]

> Speaking the truth in love, we are to grow up in every way into him who is the head, into Christ, from whom the whole body, joined and held together by every joint with which it is equipped, when each part is working properly, makes the body grow so that it builds itself up in love. (Ephesians 4:15–16)

JOURNEYING ALONGSIDE

Those words appear just a few verses after one of Paul's key teachings about spiritual gifts in Ephesians 4. In the contexts of Paul's three teaching sections on gifts (in Romans, 1 Corinthians, and Ephesians), you'll find love mentioned every time, as well as unity. On the one hand, a lot of what needs to be said as we reimagine spiritual gifts is about each of us individually as we live our journeys of gifting. But our reimagining must also envision my need for others and their needs for me in our journeys.[2]

In chapter 2 we looked at our journeys as the path of battles we need to engage because God has planned to enrich us with our gifts as spoils of those battles. His power, as our Mighty Warrior, is available to us in those battles. But it is also his will that we draw power for the battles from one another. My growth into being more authentically who I am, during the times I met with Tom and Greg, had a lot to do with the strength I developed through having that "band of brothers."

I admit to you that, because I'm an introvert, my two friends had to repeatedly chip through my protective outer layers to get to the raw Bill. But I've also noticed with my extroverted friends that I have to chip through their external presentations of themselves to get to know the raw person inside.

The business of walking alongside one another through our journeys and battles is not like falling off a log. It's much easier for us to stay at superficial levels. Many Christians seem to do that, preferring to just help each other feel better instead of the messier, scarier, and harder work of real knowing and being known. But it's at that deeper level that we'll provide one another with the help we need the most.[3]

If you want to help me fight the most important battles in my heart, your love for me will have to take the form of respectful but persevering digging to discover my potentials and obstacles. Your love for me will have to be patient and devoted. And to help you fight your most important battles, that's what you'll need from me.

As we continue to reimagine spiritual gifts in this chapter, we're broadening our understanding of the topic by acknowledging what the scriptures around gifts are describing: that an environment of sincere love is strategic for the discovery and development of our gifts.

If I think I can manage my gift discovery and development all by myself, I'm very mistaken. Reading a book about it isn't sufficient (including this one). Taking a class about gifts doesn't cut it. Taking a spiritual gifts test or inventory falls short. Even my solo studying of Scripture isn't enough.

I need you. I need the dynamic of us, with truth working in love, in real time. It's not that the cognitive inputs from these other sources aren't useful. They can be very useful. But a power that surpasses those comes from our togetherness in sincerity.

SINCERE TOGETHERNESS

Ephesians 4:1–16 intertwines discussion of our growth with our gifting. Paul also connects our gifts with our growth in Romans 12. He exhorts us to be involved in ongoing transformation of ourselves (12:1–2), and then describes the first way this will be displayed: gifted diversity (12:3–8).

- "Be transformed by the renewal of your mind" (12:2).
- "Think [of yourself] with sober judgment, each according to the measure of faith that God has assigned" (12:3).
- "We, though many, are one body in Christ, and individually members one of another. Having gifts that differ . . ." (12:5–6).

If we were to read Romans 12:1–2 by itself, about offering our bodies as living sacrifices and being transformed by the renewing of our minds, we might think we are being assigned a solo task. But the rest of the chapter focuses on me interacting with others. It's about having an accurate self-concept amid a diversified body (12:3–8) and sharing sincere love with one another (12:9–21). The implication is that we need one another in our journeys of transformation.

Just seeing one another each Sunday and catching up with our life events doesn't meet this need. At a deeper level, you have the need to share with me how you're doing at becoming transformed and renewed from the inside out, and I need to trust you with the same insights about myself. We call this vulnerability, for the purpose of our growth.

Now the me that is knowing you at that level and the you that is knowing me at that level are quite different from one another. Why? Because we are gifted so differently. If I'm thinking more highly of my gifted self than I'm thinking of your gifted self (12:3), our togetherness has hit a snag, and we'll be helping one another with a less sincere love than Scripture calls us to.

So "love must be sincere," Paul says (12:9). I am called to be devoted to you and honor you (12:10). This is one of the great ways I have been loved by others in my life. I have experienced up-close devotion and honor from a small number of close friends throughout my life. It's important because I tended to seesaw from having an estimation of myself that was too high, to having an estimation of myself that was too low.

The sincere love of a few fellow-journeyers was what it took for me to learn to value the gifted man I am without comparing myself, favorably or unfavorably, to others. We all need that. We need sincere togetherness with one another in order to grow into the balanced realization, development, and use of our potentials.[4]

Spiritual gift development is a together journey. I do not gain the benefits of that together journey in superficial or short-term relationships because those do not touch my soul. The power of your belief in me is transferred to me by gradual, up-close osmosis.

Therefore, it doesn't happen in a four- or six-week class on spiritual gifts, and probably not in a twelve-week small group with no ongoing substantial relationships. When I have guided small groups in learning the Journey View of gifts, I've led them through twenty-six weeks (six months) of study and relating. That's because our assimilation of scriptural truths needs the context of a sincere love that becomes powerful in our hearts over time.

GETTING SPECIFIC ABOUT LOVE

As we saw in chapter 3, we're fortunate that one of Paul's presentations about gifts is to a church with prominent problems, Corinth. Perhaps because of that, when Paul again links spiritual gifts with love, he gives a detailed description of love in 1 Corinthians 13. This description is a gold mine for us because it lists particular characteristics of love that we can use to evaluate how we're doing at loving, whether as groups or as individuals.

Paul wants his readers to go deeper than just head knowledge about gifts. Through his switch from the Corinthian-preferred Greek term *pneumatika* (spiritual expressions) to the term *charismata* (grace-expressions), he wants to focus them on God's grace[5] in and among one another. He wants them to experience that grace, collectively and interpersonally.

Through his presentation of the body metaphor, he invites them to imagine themselves as a united whole representing Christ. And, as we saw in chapter 3, this letter addressing all the problems of the Corinthians, including disunity related to diverse gifting, is headlined with the image of the cross—the image of profound grace and love.

Therefore, he goes deeper—he gets nitty gritty—about what love will look like (13:4–7) as he speaks to people more focused on being impressive and impressed (13:1–3). The qualities of love Paul lists are most often applied in a general way to any relationships, from marriage and family to church fellowship, to friendships with our neighbors and coworkers in the world.

Certainly, they are important for all of those. But in 1 Corinthians 13, Paul unpacks the details about sincere love specifically as an antidote to relational dysfunctions around spiritual gifts. These words, therefore, form a road map for us as we seek to build relationships that encourage healthy spiritual gift development in one another.

We already saw that Paul, in Romans 12, challenges us to love each other with devotion and honor. 1 Corinthians 13:4 breaks that out with more detail, listing love's qualities of patience and kindness, and its lack of jealousy and pride. If I want to, in powerful ways, help you grow into your potentials (gifts) and deal with your obstacles to that growth, I need to understand just how each of these qualities will look in that kind of relationship.

EVALUATING OUR LOVE

To apply each of love's characteristics in my relationship with you, I need to a) receive you as a person of value, and b) nurture you with affirmations and challenges. I am suggesting that each facet of love listed in 1 Corinthians 13 can be applied in a Valuing way and a Nurturing way.

Valuing is the side of love where we show that we *receive* the other person as they are. We communicate that we value them as a beautiful expression of God on his spectrum of grace. Nurturing is the side of love where we *give* to another the affirmations and challenges they need. We encourage and exhort them to fight the battles in their journeys of growth.

The Greek word for love used in 1 Corinthians 13 is *agape*. Worksheet 1 (at the back of this book) has an Agape Evaluation you can use to evaluate your love, or a small group can use to evaluate the group's ways of relating. For each quality of love, the Agape Evaluation clarifies how that aspect of love would receive someone in a Valuing way and give affirmation or challenge in a Nurturing way.

For example, the first quality of love listed in Paul's description is patience. My patience with you is strategically important if I am going to learn who you are at a more than superficial level. This has a lot to do with good listening, and high-quality listening requires patience.

Perhaps I do not do a good job listening to you and learning more deeply who you are because I am a person conditioned by my fast-paced, high-tech society, so my attention span is brief. Or, for a variety of reasons, you may be a challenge to my patience as I try to listen to you.

But patience, and each of these characteristics, is a strategy of love to help you grow into your giftedness. My goal in valuing you through patience is that you would feel listened to, which can help you learn to value who you authentically are. Also, as I patiently listen to you, I gain a more accurate understanding of who you are.

Patience also nurtures with affirmations and challenges, but it waits for the right moments to do so. Then, when the time is appropriate to affirm or challenge, patience guides me to make my words fit your current need rather than generically dispense to you what I think is my "wise insight" about your life.

How am I doing at loving in these ways? How is our group doing at this?[6] Use the Agape Evaluation as a tool to assess your strengths and weaknesses in loving and to chart a path into higher quality loving. We've touched on the first quality evaluated in the Agape Evaluation—patience. This tool likewise helps you evaluate yourself in each of the qualities mentioned in 1 Corinthians 13.

One reason I've focused on listening here is because it is one of the most basic skills we need to use to lovingly help each other grow into our gifted potentials. Fundamentally, I need to believe in my value if I am going to travel the journey of my gifting.

Through sincere listening, you can powerfully communicate to me that I am valued. If you listen to me poorly, you may be adding to the message that I am not of much value and contribute another obstacle to my growth. Due to this strategic nature of listening, chapter 8 will be devoted to it.

CLOSING THOUGHTS

As you study the concepts in the Agape Evaluation—each of the 1 Corinthians 13 qualities—realize that each of these are both ways you need to give love and ways you need to receive love. Together they describe an ideal community that offers to each of us support in our gifting journeys. You can also use these explanations of love to learn wisdom about people whose love for you is or is not trustworthy, while always remaining humble that you are not yet perfect in your loving.

In this life we will never achieve ideal communities of perfect loving, but Scripture's descriptions of perfect love can serve as a north star to keep moving toward. We fall short in loving because we are all still in process in developing maturity (Ephesians 4:13). This is another reason why our studies of spiritual gifts need to be linked with deepening spirituality in each of us. For my love to grow more sincere, it needs to keep developing deeper roots into the love of God within me.

In this chapter, I've emphasized how important love is. But I don't want you to draw a wrong conclusion from that—too narrow of a conclusion. *Agape* is the prescribed environment for each person's development of potential. However, in God's wisdom, adverse—even hostile—circumstances can form a context for growing into our gifted uniqueness. We'll be looking at that in chapter 7.

In 1 Corinthians, teaching about the grace-expressions we call spiritual gifts, Paul points us to a core reality ("the most excellent way," 12:31 NIV) without which all the gifts are just a lot of noise (13:1–3). The way of love and grace for one another is what matters.

These passages about gifts, in their contexts, were never meant to focus us on abilities we get, but on unique people growing together into an amazing display of God's spectrum of grace.

As I read about the specific qualities of love we need to share with each other in that process, I learn that I need grace from you, and you need grace from me. That will look like patience, forgiveness, believing in each other, and so on. It's all quite personal. This grace comes to us through each other's faces, ears, voices, and loving presence.

As God's grace (*charis*) is incarnated through us for one another, we are empowered to keep growing into the grace-expressions (*charismata*) he's created us to be. In part 2, we will look more intently at that journey in its various dimensions.

FOR REFLECTION AND LISTENING

*Powerful relating consists in grasping
a vision of what God has in mind for someone....
And a godly vision releases giddy excitement
when someone moves toward it, even just a little.*

—LARRY CRABB[7]

1. What are the challenges and fears you face in being vulnerable (speaking the truth) about your life, as described in this chapter, with a few trusted friends?

2. What would it be like for a friend to love you with "giddy excitement" as she or he sees you moving toward expressing your gifted potential? What would it be like to share that loving excitement with a friend of yours who is growing into their potential?

3. As you consider 1 Corinthians 13 and the Agape Evaluation (worksheet 1), where do you think your growth points are in learning to love effectively?

PART TWO

WALK THE JOURNEY

In part 1, we surveyed the high peaks of the Journey View of spiritual gifts. Spectrum of grace, the spoils journey, cross wisdom, and powerful love are themes that work like a compass to orient us to the biblical landscape we stand in as we take in the panorama of spiritual gifting.

But if you or I, or someone we're walking alongside, wants to forge a path into that landscape, what would that involve? How do these themes of the Journey View work out in the day-to-day life of an individual? How does this different perspective on gifts discovery, development, and use look in the realities of someone dealing with life's obstacles and opportunities?

Meet Jaden, a young adult Christian with obstacles and opportunities. And meet me, his pastor, who will provide guidance for Jaden's journey and learn some lessons of my own along the way. In part 2, we'll take the four high peaks of the Journey View and translate them into story.

CHAPTER FIVE

IMAGINE YOUR INHERITANCE

To begin and empower your journey into developing your gifted potential, you need a vision of where you're headed. Gifts-as-spoils are part of the bigger vision of you as a rich heir in Christ.

JADEN'S EMPTINESS

I studied Jaden's numb expression across the small table, the steam from our coffees rising between us. A coffee shop is usually not the place to have a discussion that goes beyond our outside appearances. But the patrons were few and far between at this midafternoon time. Through his honesty with me at our previous meeting, Jaden invited me to join him as he finally faced the emptiness in his life.

That first conversation happened in my office at church. Our growing youth ministry needed more staff, and Jaden agreed to meet and talk about coming on board to work with teens. Jaden appeared to me to be a solid young adult Christian, loving husband and father, and gifted in connecting with young people. So that earlier meeting in my office started out with a focus on those appearances:

Me: "I know you've been meeting with Rashad and Jon for, what is it, a couple years now?"

Jaden: "It'll be two years in September. Yeah, it's been good. I like those guys, and it's helpful to have some men who care about me. We can study the Bible together, check in about family and stuff. Yeah, it's all good."

Me: "That's great. I've found those kinds of relationships are essential for me because they'll speak truth when I need challenge, but love and accept me through it all."

Jaden: "Absolutely, Pastor."

Me: "Just call me Bill. So you and Kimberley have been married for how long?"

So went the conversation, covering highlights of family, church, work, salvation, hobbies, and so on. But then I continued:

Me: "People who work effectively with youth are a special breed. Out of their hearts they want to touch the lives of young people to share the amazing love and power of Christ so those kids can find a solid foundation for launching into life. They need that badly with all the craziness and temptations in our society today. Tell me about God's love and power at work in your life, and how you could see yourself sharing that with our youth."

Jaden began to stumble with his words. He went back to saying it was good to study the Bible in the men's group. He and Kimberley prioritized time together, and he spent quality time with his small daughter and son. His work colleagues experienced him as honest and caring. But the words I heard seemed more like the reciting of a grocery list than the sharing of a vital and authentic relationship with God that could be enthusiastically and contagiously shared with youth.

I had a decision to make at that point. Do I follow my gut and probe deeper into Jaden's heart? Or do I go with the satisfactory appearances, step through the recruiting process, and seal the deal to fill the ministry slot? Or try to do both?

The decision I made in my office that day led to meeting at this coffee shop five days later. In my office, Jaden admitted he didn't know what to say about God's love and power being active in his life. That though he felt his salvation was real, he was just checking off the boxes when it came to living as a Christian. His words were tentative, and his spirit subdued. But he also, in owning up to this hollowness, seemed to display courage from deeper in his heart.

My decision was to say, "I hear you talking about your Christian activities and efforts. But I don't think I'm hearing about you really experiencing God's love and power. Would you be willing to tell me more?" Jaden's acknowledged need, and my desire to see him grow into the man God made him to be, coincided in our agreement to meet again. Setting aside the ministry need for the time being, I shifted focus to the need before me in my Christian brother.

The numbness on Jaden's face over our coffees didn't prevent him from telling me more. In fact, he seemed to need to. Jaden revealed to me that his life, exterior and interior, wasn't integrated around a single core. Who he was at church, and even in his marriage, was not his whole story.

Jaden was trying to fill the vacuum in his heart in a variety of ways, leading to dis-integration in his life. He kept all that hidden.

But when I asked him to tell me more and let him know I would be a safe listener, he felt invited to speak truthfully.

Even his two years of fellowship with Rashad and Jon fell short of dealing with the truth in love. Jaden had a lot to say, both about his efforts to fill his hollowness and his heart's struggles to relate to God, his wife, and others. The conversation led to three or more cups of coffee.

As I drove away from that listening session with Jaden, I had two thoughts on my mind. First, here's a Christian who is out of touch with the hope, riches, and power that are his as a child of God. And second, if I don't pay attention to the spiritual maturity level of a gifted person I'm matching to a ministry, I'm not effectively serving them or the people they will serve.

THE BOTH / AND

If we want to help people experience fulfilling ministry to others, and have genuine impact through that service, our recruitment contacts need to go deeper than spiritual gift identification and ministry matching. Many Christians are floundering or just going through the motions. Some of them know it, and some don't. Jaden was kind of in the middle on that.

An easy way to hide what's missing is to keep busy. Pastors may unintentionally add to that truth-covering busyness as we recruit people into ministry. My contacts with Jaden needed to be less about staffing and more about Jaden. Bottom line: I wanted Jaden to be able to powerfully touch teens' lives from a restored heart unleashed through his gifts. So the restored heart had to come first.

Am I saying we must focus on responding to the human brokenness in those we serve, ignoring the need to involve Christians in important ministries to others? We all know that's impractical. Thank God for the ministries of our churches, and that we imperfect people can meaningfully serve through them with positive impact.

But perhaps it's a both/and, and perhaps we need to reframe the issue. What if we were to connect the spiritual growth of Christians with their gifted ministry better than we have?

In my own ministry career, I've served as a pastor, chaplain, and leader of intensive growth workshops. I can see how my journey of psychospiritual[1] development led to increasingly effective ministry through those roles. I progressively moved from tangible brokenness toward healing and integration as I stepped into who I am in Christ.

We want people to share and enjoy serving in ministries, in sync with their spiritual gifts. If we want to see that happen, not just because of successful ministry matching, but also as an outflow of hearts experiencing hope, riches, and power in Christ, what would we do differently?

It begins with having a vision of the amazing identity God gives to each Christian. It's a vision that encompasses God's commitment to the growth and healing we all need and the ways we're each uniquely designed (gifted) to serve others. What is that vision?

THE BIG PICTURE: INHERITANCE

Let's note first that integrating the ministries of Christians with their spiritual growth is God's plan, out of the vision in his heart. God sees how Jaden is both defeated in his own soul and neutralized as an effective servant in God's kingdom—including in his local church.

And in grace, God responds. He responds with a vision, a plan, and a promise. God intends to restore Jaden. How does God intend to do that?

In chapter 2 we discovered Paul's Ephesians 4:8 hyperlink to the Old Testament story of God gifting his people with spoils along their journey. The many stories of Israel reaping spoils from vanquished foes are close-up snapshots of the bigger picture of the inheritance God promised to them.

Even today, the phrase "the promised land" describes a wonderful life and society and creates in us yearning for it. The concept comes from the Old Testament story, which begins with God's vision of a people of his own. When God made that vision very particular by choosing one man and his descendants, God made a promise. He promised an inheritance to Abraham, Isaac, and Jacob.

The inheritance was a land, and security and prosperity in that land if they continued in faithful relationship to God. His people set their sights on that inheritance, believing in its reality as they looked back on God's promise and looked forward to the promised riches. Then they got busy fighting battles and reaping the spoils along the journey.

What does that have to do with Jaden and with recruiting him to use his gifts to work with youth? His gifts are strategic for use in youth ministry. But his gifts are also rich spoils buried within himself.

Jaden is like Israel. God's people experienced deliverance from Egypt, yet enemies still possessed their inheritance. Jaden had been saved, but the riches God has for him—the powerful unleashing of his gifted self—still needed liberation from the corruptive effects of sin.

IMAGINE YOUR INHERITANCE 55

To engage the battles to reap those spoils, Jaden must start by cultivating within himself a deep belief in God's promised inheritance for him. To engage with his growth into the powerful ways God has gifted him, he must imagine in his soul that God has a promised land for him.

Is this Old Testament imagery and story relevant to New Testament Christians and their growth and gifts? It's interesting that a few chapters before Paul's gifts-as-spoils hyperlink in Ephesians 4, he's writing to Christians about inheritance. In Ephesians 1, Paul enthusiastically proclaims to us a vision of ourselves as rich heirs! He makes clear we are rich heirs in Christ because of the gracious intention of God's will (Ephesians 1:3–14).

As heirs, Paul prays that our hearts would be bursting with hope, riches, and power (1:15–19)! What if Jaden came to believe in himself as a rich heir in Christ? What if, in the hope of this vision, he began growing in this grace and reclaiming his rich but muted potentials? What if that all flowed into powerful ministry with young people? What if this is what matching gifted people with ministries is really about?

This is the mighty working of God. In both the Old and New Testament, he proclaims an inheritance, chooses heirs, and dazzles us with descriptions of his people enjoying the riches. But the New Testament promises involve a power source beyond those in the Old. Paul assures us that the hope, riches, and power given to Christians by God are given . . .

> According to the working of his great might that he worked in Christ when he raised him from the dead and seated him at his right hand in the heavenly places, far above all rule

and authority and power and dominion, and above every name that is named, not only in this age but also in the one to come. And he put all things under his feet and gave him as head over all things to the church, which is his body, the fullness of him who fills all in all. (Ephesians 1:19–23)

The power of the risen Warrior Christ is ours as we set our sights on his inheritance for us! We can engage the battles for our spoils because he has faced our enemies and already defeated them. The Christ who descended to lead the way into our battles has ascended to his throne victorious, leading the vanquished enemies in his train. Because we are heirs, his victorious ascent showers upon us the rich gifts-as-spoils he always intended as our inheritance.[2]

Grace was given to each one of us according to the measure of Christ's gift. Therefore it says, "When he ascended on high he led a host of captives, and he gave gifts to men." (In saying, "He ascended," what does it mean but that he had also descended into the lower parts of the earth? He who descended is the one who also ascended far above all the heavens, that he might fill all things.) (Ephesians 4:7–10)

Paul envisions Christ's ascent as inheritance-empowering (Ephesians 1) *and therefore gift-giving* (Ephesians 4). Jaden needed this vision, both of himself and of his victorious Warrior Christ. We each need this vision of inheritance and spoils. Christians have been delivered, yet the journey of removing our gifts from the corruptive effects of sin lies before us, needing our engagement. Our starting point for engaging with this process is this vision of ourselves as rich heirs. Now let's check in with Jaden.

JADEN DEVELOPS A VISION

Jaden's willingness to let someone know the struggles he faced paid off. We met a few more times, and it became obvious he desired more than the routine Christian life he was living.

Sitting outside a café one Tuesday morning, enjoying scones and cappuccinos, I asked him, "What's going on, Jaden? I see something different on your face than I saw in our first couple meetings."

Jaden: "Yeah! Man, I was in a fog for so long! Maybe I was depressed. I don't know. But I definitely felt no enthusiasm for life. I think I was stuck in an endless loop. Like some computer virus attacked the software in my brain."

Me: "Isn't that amazing? From a distance you looked like you were doing okay."

Jaden: "Well, I wanted you, the church, or whoever to think that. I guess I just mimicked the other Christians around me so I would be accepted by them. And for Rashad, Jon, and my wife to look up to me! It's strange though—playing those games, I was trying to fill my emptiness with pleasures and material stuff. I was living as a fake, Bill. Showing people around me a fake Jaden and running after fake treasures."

Me: "Wow. So you think God has something better for you?"

Jaden: "I do, Bill! I feel hope. Y'know, all those sermons and Bible words about God doing amazing stuff in me and then using me to make a big difference in people's lives? Those didn't mean anything to me before. I'm starting to think there's something to it. To the idea that my true treasure is who I am in God through Jesus. And I want to thank you."

Me: "Thank me?"

Jaden: "Yeah. I guess I thought that, when you first asked to meet to talk about youth ministry, you'd just find out if I was willing to serve and—bam!—I'd be hanging out with teenagers and having a blast. But you must have seen through my façade. You invited me to tell the truth about my life. And these last couple times we've met, you challenged me to believe that God values me as his son—an heir with Christ!"

Me: "You're making me smile, Jaden! You're a man with wonderful gifts, and I see now, better than before, how you'll be amazing in serving our youth! But the world does offer all these fake treasures. We often take our eyes off the true riches—including the rich gifts God put within each of us to develop and enjoy and use to bless others."

Jaden: "Bill, I know that if I get with God's program for me, if I follow my new passion for him, he can use me uniquely in the lives of young people."

Question: Am I recruiting Jaden? Or am I discipling Jaden? Or is it a both/and?

I have invited Jaden to—in his words—"get with God's program." That program will involve both growth and gifted ministry: two intertwined priorities God has for Jaden, and for each one of us. Of course, it's more than a "program." It's the victorious and ascended Christ delivering us and showering us with grace-gifts. It's Christians growing in their hope, riches, and power as heirs with Christ. Jaden has begun to imagine that inheritance.

FROM DAMAGE TO RESTORATION

We began our reimagining of spiritual gifts (in chapter 1) by envisioning God's spectrum of grace (1 Peter 4:10). But the spectrum has been damaged. Our display of God and his grace, through our gifted diversity, is corrupted by sin's effects in all of us. Jaden's discovery, development, and use of his gifts is held hostage until he is growing in the grace and knowledge of Christ.

When I started going deeper with Jaden, sin's damage in him was exposed. It's never encouraging to look at that damage, whether in ourselves or others. But we learned in chapter 2 that, when we fail to move into the rich inheritance God has for us, he responds in grace: "I will restore your fortunes!"

The gifted ministries of God's people can be amazingly powerful in our churches and world, but it depends on the working of God's restorative grace in Christians' hearts. Matching gifted people to ministries, if it is not integrated with that restorative work, will lack powerful effectiveness.

God's promises of inheritance and restoration were the encouragement I needed to go to the level of real with Jaden as I sought to match him to ministry. Then I could contagiously convey that encouragement to him. He needed that, for ahead lay his battles in the process of growing and retrieving his gifts. In chapter 6, we turn our attention to those battles.

FOR REFLECTION AND LISTENING

> *We have lived for so long with a "propositional" approach to Christianity we have nearly lost its true meaning. . . . For centuries prior to our Modern Era, the church viewed the gospel as a Romance, a cosmic drama whose themes permeated our own stories and drew together all the random scenes in a redemptive wholeness.*
>
> —BRENT CURTIS AND JOHN ELDREDGE[3]

1. Jaden is being invited into the "cosmic drama" of being an heir in Christ. He's invited to follow his ascending Christ into the journey of discovering his rich spoils. How is this different than the usual teaching about discovering and using your gifts?

2. How have you seen that your personal potentials to make an impact are tied to your growth? How have you seen in others that discovery and use of spiritual gifts is dependent on spiritual growth?

3. Imagining yourself as a rich heir in Christ propels you into the spoils (gifting) journey. How would you be changed if you imagined yourself and your story using these biblical images?

CHAPTER SIX

ENGAGE YOUR BATTLES

Within you, there are enemies to your journey into your gifted potential. You must choose to engage those battles in your growth. As you imagine the true you God intends you to be, you can be pulled forward through the battles in your gifting journey.

This book suggests a paradigm shift in how we think about spiritual gifts. One aspect of that shift is from seeing gift-receiving as a passive event at a point in time to seeing it as an active pursuit in a person's journey of growth.

This idea that gifting is a progressive experience is based on a) understanding New Testament statements about gift-giving and receiving as metaphorical rather than concrete, and b) seeing how gifts are integrated with growth in the Epistles, and how that is illustrated through Paul's intentional link to spoils-as-gifts in Old Testament story (Ephesians 4:8; also see chapter 2). These interpretations are explained and supported in chapters 12 through 15.

The Journey View, therefore, draws our focus to people in process, rather than the automatic addition of new abilities. And it suggests that gift discovery and development is not only progressive, but also contingent. Applied to life, this means that battles, trials, and obstacles in our journeys are strategic factors for developing giftedness.

Let's see how this applies in Jaden's story.

JADEN'S NEED

Through paying attention to Jaden, I've discerned in him more of his potentials to serve in ministry. Before, he just seemed like a guy who would be good to work with youth. Now I was enjoying his curious sense of humor, hearing about his natural musical ability, and watching how he pivoted from those to sincerely and simply lay out truth someone needs to hear.

However, Jaden needed spiritual development to become an effective servant. His spiritual gifts were already in his DNA. But the more a person lacks in psychospiritual maturity,[1] the more their gifts will be hidden, dormant, stunted, misdirected, or misused. Jaden's gifts were layered over with various unresolved issues and immaturities.

So Jaden had his work cut out for him. Earlier, I referred to that work as "an active pursuit in a person's journey of growth." In that pursuit, to use the spoils metaphor, a person "receives" their gifts by retrieving them from enemy possession. Or we might say by "plundering" their enemies if we wanted to use Old Testament terms. But what the person is actively pursuing is psychospiritual growth and health, with gift discovery wrapped into it.

We all know that, as soon as we become intentional about spiritual growth, we face opposition. I tell people, "The truest thing about life this side of heaven is battle." The people of Israel often displayed fear, self-centeredness, idolatry, lack of faith, and lust for worldly treasures. All these and more sins obstructed pursuit of their God-given inheritance and spoils. We face similar enemies when we set out to live as God's heirs and discover his gifts in ourselves.

The unique ways God has crafted Jaden to impact others for Christ are features of his character that need his maturing to become effective. There are many battles he must face into in that growing process. Where is Jaden in that journey?

SCENES OF BATTLE

The truth-in-love balance was working. Jaden came to experience me as a spiritual mentor who would celebrate and value his unique strengths while also knowing and challenging him about his shortcomings and sins. To use 1 Corinthians 13 ideas, I was letting him know I believed in him, and connecting my rejoicing in him to his movement from unrighteousness toward truth (13:6–7).

Jaden's reception of truth in love primed him for pursuit of growth toward becoming a healthy Christian. Now Jaden would need to engage with his battles. The knock on my office door had a determined sound. In marched Jaden, with an angry look on his face.

Jaden: "There's no way I can make her happy! I don't even know what she wants!"

Of course, the "she" was his wife, Kimberley.

Me: "Tell me what's going on."

Jaden: "Bill, it seems like Kimberley doesn't really want to be close to me. After seven years and two kids and busting my rear to get us the life we want, she lives in her own world of the kids, her friends, church stuff, and her books. So what's left over for me? Not much!"

Me: "And you guys have talked about this?"

Jaden: "Mostly, I've kind of beat around the bush about it, my frustrations coming out in attitudes and anger sometimes. Then Wednesday I said, 'Listen, I don't understand. You seem distant; like I can't reach you. What's the problem?'"

Me: "What'd she say?"

Jaden: "Hardly anything! She was all tears." He rolled his eyes.

Me: "Hmm. How did that make you feel?"

Jaden: "Angry. Why can't she talk? And . . . why did you ask me how I felt? That sounds like what she used to say to me!"

Me: "So she used to try to connect with you?"

The only reason Jaden continued listening, after that question, is because he trusted my love for him. He knew I accepted him and believed in his potential.

"Jaden?" He lifted his head and looked at me. I saw confusion and weariness in his face.

Me: "Jaden, you and I began talking, a couple months ago, about how God could use you in ministry to young people. And the more we've talked about that, the more we've gotten excited together about that possibility.

"But the man you are, who God wants to use in that way, is a man standing at a fork in the road. You can choose to continue on the familiar path you've been walking, or you can dive into the challenging journey of growing into the man God designed you to be. If you choose that journey, God will show you, along the way, the battles you'll have to engage.

"Both you and Kimberley have room to grow. But she's not the enemy. God wants you to get real about areas in your own heart where you need to change. I have a feeling that if you engage with those battles, you'll become more the man your wife wants to be close to and trust, and you'll become more and more ready to be God's tool to impact others' lives."

Jaden and Kimberley needed more intensive work on their relationship than I had the time or training to provide. I referred them for counseling, touching base with Jaden every other week for a while. His willingness to continue the counseling process with Kimberley helped them grow together and build more authentic connection.

It became clear to both me and Jaden that some of his battles were with self-centeredness, not being his real self with others, fear, and having a divided heart. He and I were talking about those, and how these enemies in his heart negatively impacted his relationships and his potential to use his gifts on a team ministering effectively to young people.

It's so much easier to just encourage and support a person's use of their gifts, avoiding these messy areas. But how many ministries have less impact than they could because of battles that are being avoided within those who are serving? We'll never know. But we do often see Christians who have greatly used their gifts in ministry, with some success, exposed as having avoided inner battles they needed to face a long time ago.

All of us, whether we're a layperson like Jaden, a local pastor, or a prominent Christian leader, are gifted by God and intended to shine on his spectrum of grace. And no matter our ministry role or spiritual maturity level, we all need to stay clear about the battles we have yet to fight in our journeys of growth.

WELL WORTH FIGHTING

This is where using the biblical imagery of gifts as spoils can be strategic. Spoils are the results of battle victories. So if my spiritual gifts are spoils, what battles are associated with each area of my gifting?

I've received feedback that I'm good at providing attentive pastoral care to people: meeting people where they are, helping them feel heard, and providing a calm presence and strength in crisis situations. I enjoy serving others in those ways. Sounds like a gift, right?

Yet one great challenge for me has been fear of people, based on insecurities going way back in life. I've faced into those fears, working through my history that led to them. I had to unlearn lies and learn God's truth about myself and others. Armed with truth, I could grow in being more truly present with others, allowing my gifts of pastoral care to flow and have effect.

This scenario—about areas of battles linked to areas of gifting—is pervasive in our lives. I've watched other people who also identified and engaged with their hearts' battles. Seeing them grow and begin to serve others with great impact, I've felt amazement and joy. However, I've also seen people who seemed to have a gifted ability to serve in certain ways but kept resisting engagement with the battles they needed to fight within themselves.

That is sad because these are battles well worth fighting—and worth fighting well. They have to do with our spiritual growth, which is an explicit and implicit context whenever gifts are brought up in the Epistles. As mentioned earlier, the term "psychospiritual" also describes this journey because it is my holistic growth into becoming who God made me to be. It will involve many dimensions of my life and draw on various available resources.

In worksheet 2, you'll find a tool called "The Gifting Journey." It will help you reflect on how God has used, is using, and will use your life's trials as battles to recover your potentials. And it challenges you to think about how you engage with those battles proactively.

In order to fight well for your psychospiritual health and gifted uniqueness, you will need to consider using resources from your church, relationships, books, classes and education, counseling, seminars, spiritual formation, and more. Especially important is forging a small inner circle of peers with whom you can be vulnerable so they can love and challenge you as you discern and face your battles. Chapters 4 and 8 speak to that priority.

Pastors who seek to match gifted people with ministries must broaden their understanding of what that work entails. Lots of emphasis has been placed on defining each biblical spiritual gift and helping people identify which are theirs. If every believer is uniquely gifted, and if each of us has impediments to fully using our gifts, the question of what ways someone is gifted will largely work itself out as we guide them toward and support them in their necessary battles.

That's not to say that using tests and inventories has no place. We will look at that in chapter 16. But I am saying that we should shift our emphasis to people's real journeys rather than focusing mainly on categorizing them. In this chapter we're highlighting that such a focus on journey will mean helping people engage with their battles, to win their gifts as spoils.

A lot can be said about people's battles for growth and health. Many excellent resources address those. The topic is broad and going deeper into it is beyond the scope of this book. What I am suggesting here is that we look at our need to grow through the lens of spiritual gifting (and vice versa). While this focuses us on the negative realities of the battles we must face, I'll next mention how this approach in fact contributes a powerful positive magnet for our growth.

PULLED FORWARD

Part of the beauty and wisdom of each of us being a unique hue on God's spectrum of grace (1 Peter 4:10, see chapter 1) is that it points to the importance of each of us becoming who God intended us to be. None of us are fully there yet; we're on this journey we've been learning about—the journey of battles and gifting. God desires that we would each, in this life, be moving toward our full, unique expression of himself. We are each to reflect him like no one else can.

C. S. Lewis wrote of God's grace propelling us toward that uniqueness:

> That unfathomed bounty whereby God turns tools into servants and servants into sons [and daughters], so that they may be at last reunited to him in the perfect freedom of a love offered from the height of the utter individualities which he has liberated them to be.[2]

The spoils journey we have discerned involves the progressive liberation of the parts of ourselves that have been in enemy hands, moving toward becoming "the utter individualities" we each are. This reflects the glory of, and brings glory to, our Creator and Redeemer.

And when do we each reach that pinnacle of being our fully authentic selves? We are given a picture of that arrival in the last book of Scripture: "To him who overcomes, I will give . . . a white stone with a new name written on it, known only to him who receives it" (Revelation 2:17 NIV).

What a fascinating and powerful truth! God has a name for me—and it is for me alone. Why is it for me alone? It sums up perfectly who I am—the me he imagined into reality when he designed and created me uniquely.[3] Our gifting journeys, including our battles and trials, are intended to progressively form us into our authentic (true) selves, who fit perfectly together in God's spectrum of grace.

An important task in our growth and healing, therefore, is each of us imagining a vision of our true selves.[4] My need on this journey is not just to face into my battles as I consider my past and present. It is also to catch a glimpse, smell a whiff, of the new name that will be given to me one day, allowing that glimpse and whiff to become longing for that day.

Lewis speaks of our longings for our "transtemporal, transfinite" destinies: "The scent of a flower we have not found, the echo of a tune we have not heard, news from a country we have never yet visited."[5]

When I hear my new name, it will resonate with my soul. Through imagining our authentic selves, you and I can begin now to feel and move toward that resonance. This comes from each of us deeply knowing our Savior's loving belief in us. Like a magnet that vision and knowledge can pull us forward as we face into the battles in our journeys.[6]

Years ago, I caught a glimpse and smelled a whiff of my new name. Loving brothers and sisters helped me in the battle just to listen to my heart, and I formed these words: "By the grace of God, I am a lovable, tender, adventurous, powerful man of God, who soars like an eagle on the breath of God." Those words are only an echo of the magnificent new name Christ will hand me one day on my white stone. But they still resonate in my heart and pull me forward on my journey.

JADEN'S CHALLENGE

We might call Jaden's approach to life the "it should all add up" approach. The speed bump he hit in his marriage disrupted this philosophy and became an opportunity for growth. Several weeks after he burst into my office, angry at his wife, we had this conversation:

Me: "Jaden, sometimes I think what I'm hearing you say is that if you check off all the boxes in your marriage, job, church, relationships, and so on, then everything in life should add up and work. What do you think?"

Jaden: "What's wrong with that?"

Me: "Have you talked with Jon and Rashad about all this?"

Jaden: "Yeah. They're supportive and all that. But . . . they kind of imply that I'm part of the problem in my marriage."

Me: "Really? What do you mean?"

Jaden: "Well . . ." Jaden chuckled and shook his head. "They think I'm hard to get to know."

Me: "What do they want?"

Jaden: "I don't know. I guess they want . . . something else. Maybe something . . . more."

Me: "How does that make you feel?"

Jaden (smiling): "There you go again! All right. Sometimes, I just feel numb to their pursuit of me. And if I'm honest, sometimes it feels scary."

Me: "Y'know, Jaden, we've talked about some of the battles you need to fight—against sins like being self-centered and having a heart that's not truly loyal to God. Checking off all life's boxes isn't drawing you close to God, or to Kimberley, or your friends. They—including God—want to connect with the real you, Jaden. And it sounds like that's a key battle for you to engage. Knowing and sharing your true self is part of the journey of growth and gifting."

It became clear to Jaden that some of his heart's main battles in growing were in the arena of relationships. His challenge was to bring his true self to his wife, seeking to know the true Kimberley; to bring his true self to his friends, seeking to know the true Rashad and Jon; and to bring his true self to his God, seeking to know God as he truly is. The arena of relationships becomes the crucible for growth toward our full potential when the fuel of truth is injected into loving relationships.

INDIVIDUAL JOURNEY

I'll mention two points as we close this chapter. First, to some of my readers it may seem that I wander far afield of the topic of spiritual gifts. I've now told you that not only are battles and spoils relevant to understanding your gifts, but a white stone with a new name is also relevant! I believe I mentioned to you, didn't I, that we would be "reimagining" spiritual gifts?

In the view presented here, which I'll further explain in part 4, spiritual gifting is a reality that is metaphorical (rather than concrete), and the gift lists are lists of category headings. I'll also present later that what is being categorized is people, not entities called gifts. In this book, we are not focusing on defining those category headings. Instead, we are examining biblical context and connections that flesh out what spiritual gifting involves in people.

I have said all this points us to a journey understanding of gifting—and those journeys involve battles to gain our restored potentials. It also encourages us to emphasize individual uniqueness over categorization of people, though, as I will address later, categorization can be a helpful tool. Again, part 4 will discuss these various concepts.

Second, when we think about Christian growth or maturing, we often focus on factors that are generally applicable to all of us. That is important. But it is also important for each of us to particularize for ourselves what Christlikeness will look like through each of us uniquely. Both angles are valid and essential. We need that balance.

Imitation disrupts that balance and avoids the battles involved in growing toward the reality of my unique name in Christ. In chapter 3 we considered how cross wisdom challenges the wrong kind of imitation of others, which interferes with each of us serving as the unique members of Christ's body that we are.

In the Romans 12 spiritual gift context, Paul exhorts us to not be conformed but transformed. The conforming there is to worldliness, but surely it includes unhealthy imitation, a dynamic that can infiltrate the church. Transformation flows into gifted diversity in Romans 12. Conformity and imitation block gifted diversity.

To be who I truly am—growing into my gifted uniqueness—will take courage because the path of that growth goes through battles. But on that path we are following our Leader, Jesus, who engaged his battles by living as his true self. It is to his example of courage that we turn next.

FOR REFLECTION AND LISTENING

> *One wise person said anonymously, "Adversity introduces us to ourselves." And adversity comes in too many forms to number.*
>
> —DAN ALLENDER[7]

1. If you were to perceive the many forms of adversity and trials in your life as battles on a journey toward restoring your gifted potentials, how would that change your responses to those trials?

2. Jaden's enemies were the sinful attitudes of his own heart, used by him to try to cope with life. Your enemies on the growth and gifting journey are in your heart. What are they?

3. Use the Gifting Journey tool in worksheet 2 to identify how you will proactively engage with your battles in your growth and gifting journey. Then imagine and journal about your goal. What words would describe the true you who will one day receive a unique name?

CHAPTER SEVEN

BE YOU LIKE CHRIST

Living your giftedness syncs with following Jesus, carrying your unique cross. This means choosing your true self over your false self and using your gifts in servanthood. You'll need strong hope and faith when that doesn't match others' expectations.

A couple of years into walking his journey of growth, Jaden was in deeper relationships with God and others. He'd been fighting the necessary battles in himself so truth in love could do its work in his heart. This growth also clarified Jaden's unique potentials (gifts), and he and I both felt he could now serve with consistency from those strengths. A year ago, he began to serve on our youth ministry team. Then Kimberley joined him six months ago.

God used Jaden's unique gift-mix of being fun, listening well to people, giving straight talk, and having a head immersed in music, both in the lives of the young men he led and in those of his ministry teammates. I came to appreciate his humble servant heart.

Recently, I marveled at this conversation in a ministry team meeting:

Antonia: "I'm not sure how to reach the girls in my small group. They're all trying so hard to be noticed by the right people and look like the latest, greatest superstar! They make me feel like they're tuned in to the real world while I'm stuck in a dark closet on the other side of the planet!"

Kyrsten: "Wow, that's hard, Antonia. Sometimes I feel like getting these kids to see how Jesus is relevant to them is a steep climb! I go home after youth group wondering what I'm doing wrong. What am I missing? Maybe I'm not cut out for this ministry!"

There was some side-to-side chatter as everybody sympathized with Antonia and Kyrsten. But before I could break in and give some guidance, we heard somebody humming while drumming with their hands. The talking died down, and we're all looking around to see where this "music" is coming from.

Jaden was sitting there, humming and drumming with eyes closed as if he was the only one in the room! After several seconds of group listening, the laughter started, and Jaden smiled and opened his eyes. "Jaden, what's up?" I asked. Looking at Antonia and Kyrsten, he started singing "Fearless" by Jasmine Murray.[1]

Then directly but kindly, he went on: "You guys are selling yourselves short. All of us here have seen your hearts. You've both been through some rugged stuff in your lives, but it's made you more real in your faith. To hear your stories is to know that God is real, and that he's a treasure worth far more than what the girls in your group are running after. I wonder if you've trusted them with your stories."

Jaden turned to his wife: "Kimberley, what do you think? You've told me you've shared your story with the girls in your group, and they're learning to trust you and connect with you."

Kimberley: "That's true. When I first started working on this team, I remember feeling like I had nothing to offer my girls. Jaden and Susan helped me believe that the story Jesus wanted to tell through me is the story he wanted those young women to hear."

On our diversely gifted ministry team, Jaden helped others see their value and exhorted them to use their gifts. I was watching cross wisdom and powerful love at work. Jaden saw and celebrated what each person brought to the team.

JESUS AND SPIRITUAL GIFTS

Cross wisdom guides us in how to serve and relate in a diversely gifted body (chapter 3), like Jaden was doing. Yet cross wisdom has another dimension. We learn about cross wisdom only because of Jesus who carried his cross. The wisdom that teaches us how to fit into the body of Christ humbly and with honor comes from Jesus, who refused to fit into others' expectations.

I was about to learn how Jaden's further growth in cross wisdom would come into conflict with *my* expectations of him. What is this other dimension of cross wisdom, and how does it relate to our journeys of gifting?

As we saw in chapter 3, Paul links spiritual gifts with the wisdom of being the body of Christ (1 Corinthians 12), which is founded on cross wisdom (1 Corinthians 1). Through these metaphors, Paul points churches, who need wisdom about their gifted diversity, to Jesus Christ.

Jesus does not usually get much mention in books about spiritual gifts. Instead, authors often focus on the Holy Spirit[2] and tend to isolate the scriptures about gifts into their own special arena. But if we keep the passages on gifts within the tapestry of the rest of Scripture, its threads will guide us to a Jesus-centered focus.[3]

We've looked at Paul's picture of the ascending Christ giving us our spiritual gifts as spoils of victory (Ephesians 4:7–10), and how that illustrates that gifting is a journey. *Now we will see that it is the cross-carrying Christ we are to follow in our journeys as we each grow and serve with our gifted uniqueness.*[4]

We will consider this cross-carrying foundation for gifted uniqueness in two scriptures: Jesus' invitation in the Gospels to take up our crosses (Mark 8:34), and exhortations for us in Hebrews that are based on his cross-focus (12:1–2).

UNIQUE MISSION

"If anyone wishes to come after me, he must deny himself, and take up his cross and follow me" (Mark 8:34 NASB). Our Lord was intently focused on his mission. We see that throughout the Gospels in choices like these and others:

- his itinerant lifestyle
- his desire to limit his popularity
- his rebuke of disciples who misunderstood his purpose
- his rejection of resistance or deliverance during his suffering
- his refusal of an earthly kingship

What mission caused Jesus to make these choices? Just before his invitation to take up our crosses and follow him, he states he is going to suffer and be killed before rising again (Mark 8:31). His mission was his cross. Jesus clearly identified that mission in his own mind and it governed his life choices.

Jesus' cross mission was unique to him. It sprang from who he uniquely is—the Son of God and Son of Man who would become the Savior for the world. No one else ever had, nor could have, that mission. As his mission sprang from his identity, so ours do as well. And he calls each of us to take up our crosses.

My cross is unique to me, and yours is unique to you. The missions we each have in our lives spring from our unique identities. Christ calls each of us to, like himself, be clear about who we are and what our missions are.[5] He endorses your uniqueness, calls it valuable, and invites you to the adventure of living out who you are gifted to be.

TRUE AND FALSE SELVES

Calling it an adventure makes it sound glorious, doesn't it? It is glorious, and Jesus wants you to feel inspired by his call to identify and live your unique mission. Yet this call, which comes to you in his voice still today, is an invitation to your cross and a summoning to deny yourself. How can this affirmation of—and invitation to—my uniqueness also be a requirement that I deny myself?

Starting with his temptation by Satan and continuing through pressures he felt from friend and foe alike—to give in, go with the flow, get with the program—Jesus stuck with his mission. In his heart, he believed there was no other way—except to be who he is.

The temptation he faced was to create a false self that could more easily enjoy life by conforming to people's expectations and imitating others acceptable to the majority. That would be a false self because it would deny who he truly is. Instead, he kept choosing to live his unique identity and mission.[6]

Jesus chose to be himself—by denying himself. This is a core battle for each of us: stepping into my true self as I respond to the true God, pushing aside my false self. I must be very clear about these two selves that are at war inside me, or else I'm an easy mark for the forces pressuring me to conform and imitate.[7]

How can I be the brilliant unique hue I am on God's spectrum of grace if I do not identify and live as my true self? How can I be the unique part of Christ's body I am if I'm enamored with others who are celebrated, working hard to imitate them? How can I be, for people in this world, an invitation to God's grace, if I'm striving to conform to their parameters for me? Jesus asks me to deny that false self.[8]

This is the other dimension of cross wisdom. Knowing and choosing my cross is knowing and choosing my true self.

Yet as I rise above the blandness of my false self, I am kneeling down to serve. As I choose the freedom to live as the true me, I make self-limiting choices like Christ did. The mission to be your unique self blends with the mission to serve others. Blending these two aspects of life mission is part of your journey of growth.

Your spiritual gifting is about being the unique you and about bringing the unique you to others in servanthood to them.[9] It is about choosing the true you over the false you that would prefer the easier path of conforming and imitating. And your spiritual gifting is about living on mission and accepting the sacrifices that involves.[10]

We've always realized that the spiritual gifts of the body of Christ teach us about our unity amidst our diversity. What we haven't emphasized is how that is an echo of Christ's call: be united in following me as you each carry your unique cross. Be you like Christ.[11]

Here is the parallel of gifts with cross-carrying:
- Paul: you are one body. Christ: all of you follow me.
- Paul: you are individually members. Christ: each take up your own cross.

FACING OPPOSITION

To be a cross-carrying servant like Jesus, you need certain spiritual muscles. Hope and faith are two key muscles you must strengthen. When Jesus' endurance of his cross is brought up in Hebrews 12, these two qualities are emphasized.

> Therefore, since we are surrounded by such a great a cloud of witnesses, let us throw off everything that hinders and the sin that so easily entangles, and let us run with perseverance the race marked out for us. Let us fix our eyes on Jesus, the author and perfecter of our faith, who for the joy set before him endured the cross, scorning its shame, and sat down at the right hand of the throne of God. (Hebrews 12:1–2 NIV)

Jesus maintained his intent mission focus in part because of his firm hope in joy and honor beyond his cross.[12] He is also the perfect ideal of faith in God, the peak of the witnessing list of faith heroes in Hebrews 11. We are exhorted to risk running after him as we identify and pursue our own missions amid opposition.

Faith in God's past promises and hope for joy and honor in the future propel our fidelity to live and serve as our true selves today. Hebrews was written to people shrinking back to what felt familiar and safe. The realities of opposition in our journeys tempt us to shrink back to our comfort zones and avoid risks.[13]

We should not expect to always be loved, admired, and thanked for expressing our unique, gifted identities. We should instead assume we will experience what Jesus and other heroes of faith experienced: opposition, criticism, judgment, and even persecution. We can rejoice when that doesn't happen. Yet history contains many examples of people facing intimidating circumstances who nevertheless stayed true to who they were.

We did learn in chapter 4 that a loving environment is best for discovery and development of our gifts. However, the example of Jesus and other faith heroes shows that faithfulness to our unique missions and giftedness can happen in environments of opposition, where the valuing and nurturing of love is lacking. This is possible for two reasons.

First, faith anchors us to the foundation of God's promises, and hope anchors us to a future of glory when we see Christ and he honors us with our new names (Revelation 2:17). God's Word teaches me these truths. Knowing and trusting his Word empowers me to learn and express the true self he created me to be.

Second, even when the love of others fails to value and nurture us, God's love does not fail us. Jesus had firm confidence and security in his Father's love for him, even when being tortured and executed. When others do not affirm the value that I am on God's spectrum of grace, I know that his affirmation of me is solid. I am loved for who I uniquely am.

JADEN'S UNIQUENESS

Jaden's growth and gifted ministry were a joy to watch. But outside of youth group, he and Kimberley were sometimes meeting with kids who were marginal to the group. These teens—infrequent group attenders—were a contrast to the average young person in our ministry. They were into different music and clothing, even talking differently and hanging out at places the rest of the teenagers didn't go.

Jaden gravitated to them. Dropping in at their hangouts, or grabbing a bite with them after school, he kept building relationships. I figured he was a good influence on them, but I hoped it would lead them to integrate into the youth group. After some months of Jaden and Kimberley being involved with these kids, that wasn't happening.

I avoided talking to them about it, not wanting to be critical. But in my mind, I had critical thoughts. It felt like Jaden's days of being a team player were fading. He and Kimberley were still involved with youth group activities, but I was concerned they couldn't keep up with those, plus their informal outreach.

I suppose I saw Jaden as possibly my right arm one day in youth ministry, helping relieve me of some of the burden. So I felt irritated at him for branching out beyond our program. The following conversation happened over pizza at a team meeting in my home one evening:

Me: "All right. We're headed to that concert downtown soon. Looks like it's going to be Friday the twentieth. The young people are gonna love this!"

Beckett: "Yeah! Woo hoo! Rock and roll!"

Me: "Right, Beckett. Anyway, talk to your groups about it. Have them put it on their calendars. We've got church vans lined up."

Jaden: "Hey, a question."

Me: "Yeah, Jaden?"

Jaden: "I guess I wasn't clear the concert was on the twentieth, and I've already told some of the kids Kimberley and I have been ministering to that I'll go with them to a gaming convention that weekend. I know it'll mean a lot to them for me to be there."

Pausing, I silently nodded my head, looking nowhere in particular. All eyes were on me.

Me: "Okay. Well . . . Jaden, let's talk later. Now, Antonia, you wanted to talk about an activity for young women? Tell us about it."

Later, Jaden and Kimberley stuck around while the rest of my team filtered out of the house, one by one. Eventually, just the three of us were standing in the kitchen.

Kimberley: "Can we help you clean up?"

Me: "No, it's not a problem. Susan and I will get it later."

Jaden: "I guess we should talk."

Me: "Yeah, I think you're right."

We sat down in the den.

Me: "Jaden, Kimberley . . . I know you guys have been reaching out to kids the youth group hasn't been able to reach. I'm sure that's a good investment, and I assume you've been able to build some relationships that are going to pay off spiritually. It seems, though, that our ministry to the kids who are involved is what really needs our focus. I need everyone on our team to emphasize those kids."

Jaden: "Bill—"

Me (interrupting): "Wait, I'm not done. I feel badly that the kids you're serving aren't involved in the youth group. But the ones who are, and their parents . . . Well, that's where I think the church expects us to be focusing right now. We can't reach every teen."

At that point I realized I was preaching at Jaden and Kimberley, telling them it was their job to fit in. Fit in to what? *My* expectations. *My* program.

Me: "I'm sorry. God has obviously given you hearts for the young people you've been reaching out to. And I haven't even asked you to share with me what's in your hearts and what you're seeing as you touch their lives. Listen, don't worry about the concert—it'll work out. I want to hear what God is doing through you, and we don't have time to get into it now. How about we find a time next week to meet? And my job will be to listen."

I could see Kimberley and Jaden relax when I shared those words. They thanked me, and we met the following week. Later, Jaden and I met one-on-one. I learned from listening to Jaden about the unique ways God had crafted him—the very gifts I'd previously rejoiced to see him use—which caused his heart to reach out in ministry to these marginal kids.

While Jaden still cared about the young men in his small group, he had a natural chemistry happening between him and these other kids. Jaden's off-center humor, musical likes, and ways of relating were a fit for ministry to this other group. In fact, he referred to it as a calling.

Jaden's spiritual growth included developing a more unique sense of his identity and mission in following Christ. My focus on ministry within a certain organizational structure prevented me from listening for God's development of this man as part of the organic body of Christ. We will not notice or nurture each person as a unique hue on God's spectrum of grace unless we learn to be a community of listeners. We turn to that important need next.

FOR REFLECTION AND LISTENING

A favorite theme of C. S. Lewis was that "heaven will show much more variety than hell." All our mistakes turn out to have a sameness about them. There is nothing quite as unoriginal as sin. But . . . the Spirit is inventive and the forms of grace are not repeated.

—EUGENE PETERSON[14]

1. If every Jesus follower has a unique cross/mission, what does that say about the value of our gifted human variety for advancing God's kingdom?

2. How does your false self attempt to drag you down into sameness and unoriginality, away from being an unrepeated form of grace (as Peterson wrote)?

3. How will you allow hope and faith to strengthen you to run after your cross-carrying Jesus instead of being ruled by others' expectations?

CHAPTER EIGHT

YOUR LISTENING COMMUNITY

Through attentive listening, I discover the scenes of gifting unfolding within you and can share with you my fascination and encouragement. I must apply myself to learning to be a listener and offer listening to you, especially when you're in the trials and battles of your journey.

In reimagining spiritual gifts, we are moving away from an emphasis on newly added abilities and the use of testing instruments to discern what they are. We are moving into the understanding of gifts as potentials we've always had and our journeys of growth as strategic for their development. This will also involve tweaking our understanding of what is involved in discerning our gifts, including the valuing of community over testing.

Many churches place an emphasis on building a sense of community together. Reimagining spiritual gifts will involve some reimagining of community, whether in churches or among friends. We touched on this in chapter 4, focusing on powerful love and evaluating our *agape*.

When it comes right down to it, there is a skill you and I need to hone that is indispensable for helping one another discover and develop our gifted uniqueness. It is a way of sharing high-quality love that is all too rare. It is the skill of listening.

We each need the experience of a small community that is characterized by listening. We each need to learn the ways of giving and receiving listening in a community. That's because of where the scene of gifting is. It was within Jaden, wasn't it? But I had stopped listening. The scene of gifting is in you and in me.

PAYING ATTENTION TO PEOPLE

God's spectrum of grace is not made up of spiritual gifts. It is filled with people. To where does our attention turn when we think about spiritual gifts? Because of our utilitarian approach to the topic of gifts, our attention usually turns to categorization tools and then task assignments.[1] We don't give much thought to the actual scenes of gifting. Those scenes are within each of us, and we've been exploring those scenes to this point in the book.

Categorization of people is a useful tool. Paul and Peter used it when they wrote about gifts, and we use it today. We'll think more about that in later chapters. But the scenes of gifting in you and me are a lot more exciting than cognitive categories. Noticing how the Spirit of Christ is shaping you into your unique identity—for your unique mission—is where the fascination lies.

My most important need when it comes to discovering, developing, and deploying my giftedness is not data from a test. It is not accurate ministry matches. Those have their place, but I need friends who believe in me and persevere with me. Those kinds of relationships are founded upon getting to know one another more than superficially, and that depends on listening to one another.

The biblical truth that you and I are spiritually gifted is not supposed to point us to classes and curricula. It points us to being fellow explorers as we journey together. It points us to seeking for the creativity of God's Spirit embedded in each of us. You are surrounded by individuals who are each unique fingerprints of God. Attentive listening will lead you to discovery, fascination, and opportunities to encourage and be encouraged.

You need my fascination with you. I need yours with me. Fascination is one of the forms love takes. We needed it from others as children, and we do not outgrow that need. I become fascinated with you when my search for your unique giftedness is rewarded with glimpses.

BECOMING A LISTENER

To sincerely and effectively share that we believe in one another and are fascinated by what we see, we must cultivate habits of noticing and giving attention to one another.[2] The first quality of love mentioned in 1 Corinthians 13 is patience. When you attentively listen to me, you are on a search for my unique and developing true self, and that takes your patient presence with me.

There are many obstacles to this patient listening that leads to fascination and communicates love:
- We're not born as good listeners; this trait must be learned.
- We're all naturally self-focused.
- Attention spans are short, and distractions are many.

- By default, our brains try to categorize everything and everyone.
- Forming judgments about people interferes with hearing them.
- How someone fits into our priorities obscures learning about who they are.
- Few of us have been listened to well, and we lack good models of listening.
- Most media outlets today train us not to listen, but to react.

Learning to listen to one another goes against the grain of all this. As you can see from this list, there are enemies to becoming a good listener both inside of you and all around you. Learning loving listening is possible, though, through having an environment where it is prioritized, developing specific skills for listening, and cultivating your own personal depth.

In chapter 10, as we look at values for church, we will touch on creating listening environments. Later in this chapter, we'll refer to specific listening skills. But what does cultivating your own depth mean, and how is it important for listening and our spiritual gifts?

When we looked at cross wisdom (chapter 3) and powerful love (chapter 4), I mentioned that each of those dynamics, which are necessary in the diversely gifted body of Christ, requires a deepening spirituality in us. Practicing that wisdom and love among ourselves so often comes down to how we listen to one another. To become a better listener to you, I must cultivate my own spiritual depth.

There are many wonderful books about cultivating spiritual depth. Our focus in this book is on spiritual gifting, so we will not devote space to the topic of developing depth in yourself. But if you do not cultivate that depth, your ability to listen attentively and notice God's unique creativity in others will be limited.

Attentive listening requires you to be fully present rather than scattered, distracted, and insecure. Cultivating spiritual depth includes learning how to be fully present, as well as feeling secure in being yourself. Much of the time we are not fully and securely present to others, to ourselves, or to God.

If I develop depth in my spirit, I will be able to bring my fully present self to you and truly listen and learn who you are. Then my fascination with and celebration of you can overflow out of me, leading to valuing and nurturing you as the uniquely gifted person you are.

JADEN'S LISTENING GROUP

Near our church is a technical college where thousands of young adults from our region are being trained in many fields. A handful of these students sometimes attend our church, but for the most part there is no overlap between the world of our church and the world of the tech school. In fact, area residents generally avoid contact with students there because of media reports about tech students involved in petty crimes and disturbing the peace.

Not long ago I met with Jaden, Rashad, and Jon—the group of three that was learning how to be more authentic in helping each other face and fight the battles in their lives. In our discussion, Rashad mentioned some tech-school students he encountered.

Rashad: "I was in the grocery store the other day, and in the next aisle I overheard a couple of students talking about finding a job in auto repair. Their entire conversation, though, was about money. It was how to land the job that would pay the most."

Rashad has been an auto mechanic for several years, specializing in hybrid models. He's enthusiastic about doing his job well and keeps in mind that it's about people who benefit from his services, not just nuts and bolts.

Rashad: "It bothers me to hear these young people, who are going into my field, focused only on how it will reward them."

Jon: "Man, I can relate to being bothered by those students! Felicia and I were going out to dinner last weekend, and a group of them were outside the restaurant raising a ruckus and just generally being really obscene!"

Me: "Hey, guys, remember when we were talking about tuning into one another because we want to see how God is working in each other? This could be an opportunity to find out what God is doing in Rashad."

Jaden: "Yeah. Rashad, you said you felt 'bothered' by the discussion you overheard. Tell us what you mean by that."

Rashad: "Y'know, I remember when I was fresh out of tech school, and I was just like them. For a few years I was just all about me. Making the money, buying the coolest stuff, maxing out the fun of it all."

Heads were nodding as Rashad spoke. We felt the seriousness and sincerity that we saw in his face and tone of voice.

Jon: "So what happened?"

Rashad paused for a moment. "It all crumbled. I was seeking pleasure all the time, and I royally messed up my life. That's when a friend invited me to church, and I started making some good friends."

Jaden: "You sound sad, Rashad."

Rashad: "I am sad. But not because of my past. It's because these kids are heading down the same path. They don't realize what I had to learn the hard way. It's not about serving yourself. It's about serving others." A peaceful smile spread across his face: "That's where the real satisfaction is."

Me: "You have a tender heart, Rashad. Are we hearing that you really care about these students?"

Rashad: "Yeah!"

Jon: "Rashad, I hear the caring, but it sounds like more than just caring. Are you feeling more than that?"

Rashad: "Y'know, I am. I picture myself serving these students. I feel like they need something outside of their classes that can help them see their skills are about more than money and success."

In this conversation, and the ones following it, Jon and Jaden supported Rashad as he got in touch with a passion in his heart. It all started with paying attention to Rashad's report of feeling bothered by an overheard conversation. Jon and Jaden asked Rashad to share more, and by giving him their full attention and acknowledging what they were hearing he learned that what he had to share is important.

This group of men was learning to take their connecting to a deeper level. Jon's initial reaction ("They bother me too!") shifted the focus from Rashad to himself. While there's a place for easy and fun give and take, if we never slow it down and tune in to the other person's thoughts, feelings, and wants, we will never get to know them at a truer level. And we will not invite them to know themselves at that level.

Rashad ended up buying a small building and setting up an auto repair place where people below the poverty line could get their vehicles fixed for only the cost of parts. It was open certain days of the month, and he advertised and recruited for volunteer mechanics at the tech school. As he got involved with these young adults, opportunities came up to share his own story with them and to mentor them in meaningful ways.

Of course, these three men weren't the only ones learning about powerful listening. I, their pastor, after confessing that my agenda for Jaden had been more important to me than looking for God's process of growth and gifting within him, was also learning to listen. Jaden and Kimberley, with my support, shifted their focus to outreach to the youth that were marginal to our group. God blessed that ministry and our main youth program as a result.

LISTENING ON THE JOURNEY

Listening is an important skill in all kinds of relationships and situations. But in this book, we're focusing on the discovery and development of spiritual gifts. Our interest here is listening that helps one another with that—coming alongside one another in the gifting journey.

In the Journey View of spiritual gifts, gifting is intertwined with growth. Often, I need you to listen to me when I am dealing with battles I must fight to grow. During those times, neither you nor I may see how my battles are related to my gifting; it may seem like I'm just going through hard circumstances. But if we keep in mind the spoils journey (chapter 2), we'll remember that my current trials are battles I need to face to reclaim the potentials God has put in me.

When we are listened to during our struggles, it can invite us to go to a deeper level where a) we become more aware of how we need to specifically grow, and b) we gradually develop a purposeful sense of our unique true selves. At this deeper level, we realize that our trials are not just troubles to get through. They are evidences of God working in our lives to develop us into who he made us each to be. Your attentive listening invites me to this awareness.

As Jaden and Jon gave to Rashad the gift of their listening, eventually they were hearing him describe a dream. The valuing and nurturing Rashad received from his listening community formed a context for him to turn his dream into a concrete ministry in which he served through his gifts: a servant-style repair shop staffed by the young adults he was mentoring.

HOW TO LISTEN

In order to be a good listener, it is important to pay attention and be fully present. But this is only the beginning of learning to listen. You will need to learn specific skills of good listening and practice them until they become second nature.

There are a lot of great resources available to help you learn to listen. An Internet search will point you to many of those resources. Years ago, I attended a workshop on listening, and I've been practicing ever since![3]

My purpose here is not to present comprehensive lessons on how to listen. I encourage you to seek out resources and apply yourself to specific training. Here, I will simply highlight some key points about how to listen, drawing on the training I received and still use.

First, it's important to realize what you are listening for. A helpful grid to keep in mind is that you are listening for a person's thoughts, feelings, and wants. Most of the time we restrict what we share to our thoughts. Remembering this grid will help you, in your listening, to ask for someone to share at the deeper levels of feelings and wants.[4] When Jon and Jaden probed Rashad's feelings of being bothered, combined with other feelings, he began to uncover his passion to serve people in unique ways.

Second, we need to be very concrete about learning to give someone our attention. The acid test of whether I'm being attentive to you is not whether I think I am, but whether you feel my attentiveness. Concrete behaviors, such as giving someone my uninterrupted eye contact and matching my body posture to theirs, communicate my attentiveness.[5]

Third, I need to "give you the floor." Perhaps the greatest hindrance to effective listening is our interruptions or changing the subject. Fourth, when I, the listener, do speak, I need to briefly summarize what I think I've heard so the other person can correct my understanding if needed. Fifth, I must learn to ask open-ended questions that allow the person to add whatever they want to.[6]

When I've taught these skills, sometimes I have asked groups, "What is the goal of good listening?" Usually the answer given is "to be able to really hear and understand the other person." My response to that is: "When I listen, my goal is that you would feel heard." I see pursuing understanding of you as a means to that end, rather than the end itself.

It's possible for me to listen to you and gain a decent understanding of what you're saying but do a poor job of helping you feel heard. It's very difficult to do a good job of helping you feel heard and not understand some of what you're saying in the process.

Why is helping you feel heard more important than understanding you? Because my goal in loving listening is to promote your progress in your gifting journey. As I practice the skills of attentive listening, you will probably feel valued, and are given the space to draw out of your heart feelings and wants you may not have been aware of—which does not depend on my understanding of you.

Maybe you can see why I called this the "all too rare" skill of listening. It's a lot of work! But the results of giving one another the gift of feeling heard are well worth the work. The community that gives one another this gift shares affirmation and valuing with each other. We're supported in feeling security in being our true selves, discovering our potentials (gifts), and developing confidence to pursue our missions.

In these ways, communities can rejoice in the diversity of God's spectrum of grace. Powerful listening love undercuts our tendencies to divide over our diversity because through it we are giving to and receiving from one another at a much deeper heart level than we ordinarily do.

When that happens, I will be receiving grace through your face, and you will be receiving grace through my face. We will both be reflecting the grace we've received through God's face because we have turned our faces toward his. In this spiritually deepening process, we learn to listen, becoming powerful in affirming the gifted uniqueness around us.

FOR REFLECTION AND LISTENING

> *There is nothing more harmful to the soul on its journey to God than living an unobserved life. Learning to listen with transcendent curiosity as someone tells his or her story is important. It matters. It can move someone into the presence of God. It can create the opportunity for an epiphany.*
>
> —LARRY CRABB[7]

1. Who pays attention to the scenes of growth and gifting within you? To whose journey of growth and gifting do you listen? How would you like to see more attentive listening in your relationships?

2. As you do research on attentive listening skills, in which of those skills do you need the most improvement? How will you work on developing loving listening skills?

3. What are the obstacles that keep you from having and displaying "transcendent curiosity" about what God is doing in your friend's heart and journey?

PART THREE

STRATEGIES FOR CHURCH AND WORLD

In part 1 we scanned the panorama of the Journey View of spiritual gifts, familiarizing ourselves with its high peaks. In part 2 we zoomed in on the journeys of individuals who are walking the path of gifting integrated with growth.

The first two chapters of part 3 address, primarily for church leaders, how to apply the Journey View as a church. We look at strategies in the areas of teaching, growth opportunities, fellowship, and ministry engagement.

Chapter 11 also invites you to think strategically about application of the Journey View, but it turns our attention to the world beyond church. Since, in the Journey View, we see gifts as the potentials with which we were born, unbelievers also have God-given gifts. Though they lack the indwelling Holy Spirit to energize their discovery, development, and use of their gifts, our areas of commonality with them form opportunities for gospel connections.

CHAPTER NINE

VALUES FOR CHURCH— TEACHING AND GROWTH

In chapters 5 through 8, we've considered how individuals walk the journey of gift development. In this chapter and the next, we will explore what that means for a church that wants to support individuals in those journeys.

The popular approach teaches people about gifts, tests people for gifts, and tasks people based on gifts. The Journey View, however, integrates spiritual gifting with spiritual growth—and applying it in church ministry can be both more challenging and more effective than using the popular approach.

Greater effectiveness is possible because a) maturing Christians serve with greater reliability and impact than non-maturing Christians, and b) seeing spiritual growth and gifting through the lens of uniqueness is motivational.

In *Spiritual Gifts Reimagined*, we move beyond general principles about growth to talking about your specific journey and battles. We move beyond categorizing you in a group of people who have certain gifts to helping you discover your uniqueness. Principles and categories have their places, but the prospect that spiritual growth can lead us to meaningful fulfillment—because it develops us into our true unique selves—is a powerful motivation to grow and to impact others using our gifts.[1]

Yet applying the Journey View of gifts in church ministry is also more challenging because a) the methods for doing so are more dispersed throughout the church's ministries rather than defined as certain classes, tests, and role assignments, and b) making lifelong growth an important cultural value in a church disturbs the status quo in all of us.

Applying the view of gifting taught here in a church ideally starts with buy-in from leadership that is then reflected across the church's ministries. A life-integrated understanding of gifts would be matched by an integrated church ministry approach to supporting individuals in their gifting journeys.

In this chapter and the next, we'll explore four areas of values, looking at how to prioritize them across a church's ministries. These four areas for church focus and implementation are responses to the developmental needs of people walking their journeys of gifting.

TEACHING A PERSPECTIVE

Several scriptural themes form a cognitive framework for people to understand and experience the gifting journey. We have encountered them in earlier chapters, but I list them here to highlight that teaching and preaching on these themes can help people adopt these scriptural perspectives about their own gifting journeys.

Unity in Diversity

The blending of diversity into unity was clearly a burden for Paul when he brought up the body of Christ and spiritual gifts in his Epistles.[2] The premise of this book is that spiritual gifts are not about add-ons we get and use but rather the diversity of people we are.[3] We need teaching and preaching that challenges us to relational unity, building connections with one another amid our many diverse personal dimensions.

My personal characteristics (personality, gender, race and ethnicity, interests, skills) combine to make me different than you. And my journey (age, formative background and influences, education, experiences, challenges) is different than yours.

In our experience of one another, diversity is a given; unity is not a given. Our default response to diversity is not to build unity. That is why the apostles exhorted to unity and why we still need that exhortation. They urged us to *agape*, with great specificity. They filled our vision with metaphor (body of Christ in Paul; spiritual house in Peter) to inspire us.[4]

They appealed to us to see one another differently than our default way of seeing. This goes deeper than talking about how our diverse ministry functions all work together. I need teaching and preaching that challenges me to cherish what I have in common with you when you are so different than me.[5] If I can learn to cherish that commonality, I can learn to cherish how we are each unique.

In Ephesians 4, Paul introduces spiritual gifts by imploring (NASB) and urging (ESV) us to unity (4:1). Pastors and teachers, implore and urge us to cherish our unity in our diversity. And because this is about real people and real relationships, make it concrete about your specific congregation, not just principles about theoretical unity.

Cross Wisdom

In chapter 3 we learned that we need the wisdom of Christ's cross for us to live in the wisdom of being Christ's body with its spiritual gifts. We saw this as we linked 1 Corinthians 1 and 12. Paul uses cross wisdom to address problems with stratification, separation, and imitation in the body of Christ. These Corinthian issues circled around their attitudes about spiritual gifts.

It's hard to imagine a church that would not have problems with these issues at some level, for they arise out of flawed human nature. Through the wisdom of the cross, Paul is exhorting our churches to become gatherings of the humble and mutually honoring.

Spiritual gifts display our diversity, and our default response to diversity is not to build unity. It is, instead, to devolve into stratification, separation, and imitation. Preaching and teaching about spiritual gifts needs to include lifting up the cross and its wisdom because this is a key element in how Scripture confronts those reactions to gift diversity.

Chapter 3 is more detailed in presenting the dynamics involved in cross wisdom as it addresses these church problems.

Spectrum of Grace

Another necessary perspective we need to hear taught is that we are all grace-expressions on God's spectrum of grace. Again, the starting premise of this book is that spiritual gifts are not about things we get but rather the potential-filled people we are. This argues for teaching that clarifies that the term "spiritual gift" is a beautiful metaphor for showing us that we are all unique expressions of God's grace (*charismata*).

All Christians in your church should be serving according to their giftedness, yet some are and some are not. A church can tilt toward a utilitarian response to that, encouraging members to serve and perhaps training them about their added-on abilities. Or it can tilt toward affirmation of the grace-filled uniqueness of each person and how together we form an amazing spectrum of God's grace.

Teaching that instills in our hearts that grace is on display through us individually and corporately encourages a flow of people into serving. When people see their serving as a way to uniquely display God's grace through each of them, opportunities to serve are more enticing. Pastors and teachers, entice us to this flow of grace!

We also need teaching that entices us to wonder at God's spectrum (*poikilos*) of grace and wisdom. In chapter 1, we contemplated the prism of God's grace and how our hearts need to be captured by the brilliancy of the vast and variegated spectrum of hues God's grace has created. We could all easily list many negative or ho-hum attitudes toward church among both Christians and non-Christians. Pastors and teachers, paint for us the picture of this spectrum God finds beautiful and breathtaking!

Scriptural Story

I quoted Dan Allender earlier: "The Bible assumes that its stories are also our story."[6] As pastors and teachers, we often focus on Old Testament stories of individuals whose journeys inspire us to faith and fidelity to God. But what have we taught our people about the value of the Old Testament battle stories that Paul points to when he speaks of spiritual gifts in Ephesians 4:8?

Paul's Psalm 68 citation is like Lewis's wardrobe,[7] which ushers us into a story-filled panorama where our gifts are the spoils of battles and victories to which God invites us. While some authors on spiritual gifts include information on how our spiritual growth relates to our gifts,[8] we need teaching that integrates our discovery, development, and use of our gifts with our battle-filled journeys.

When Paul says that gifting has been seen before, pointing to the journey of God's people into the promised land, we get a graphic picture of the spiritual growth Paul connects with gifts in his letters. We learn that gifting is dependent on victories in our growth. He clearly tells us our gifting hangs on Christ's victory, then points us to people (in the Old Testament) who could only share in gifts-as-spoils through obedience in following God into battles (Ephesians 4:8–10).

I need to hear preaching and teaching that recasts the trials and challenges of my life into battles that are necessary for me to develop into the fullness of my identity and potential (my promised land). Pastors and teachers, fill our minds with the metanarrative that invites us to find our journeys in biblical story. Appendix 2 lists the scriptures that develop the Old Testament spoils theme.

Unique Mission

In chapter 7 we followed the thread of cross wisdom (from 1 Corinthians) to Jesus' focus on his cross as his unique mission. He calls us to our own unique missions, requiring sacrificial denial of our false selves and unity in following in his steps (Mark 8:34).

In the popular ability-centered view, it is hard to see much relevance of Jesus' example to spiritual gifts.[9] If our view of gifts instead emphasizes that we're all unique potential-filled people, Jesus' example and call to follow takes on crisp relevance to spiritual gifts.

Teaching that links Jesus' cross-focus to our gifts will emphasize several themes, previously discussed in chapter 7:

- The identification of your cross/mission is strategic for your life and arises out of saying yes to your unique true identity, as it did for Christ.
- You must say no to pressures from others and from yourself to live as a false you, which will require sacrifices.
- Your faith in what God has said and your hope in the future he promises must be strengthened for living your unique mission.
- Keep your eyes on Christ, moving toward your journey's climax, when he will clarify your unique identity by giving you your new name.

Jesus calls us to the diversity of our gifted uniqueness, while united together in following him. Our gifted diversity needs a Christocentric focus. Pastors and teachers, call us to this life-transforming focus!

This list of themes for teaching is not exhaustive. The view of gifts taught here sees spiritual gifts as part of the fabric of Scripture from Genesis to Revelation. The themes mentioned are important highlights and are developed in more detail in preceding chapters.

ENCOURAGING PERSONAL GROWTH

We've looked at the cognitive support teaching provides as we walk our gifting journeys. We also need developmental support. I need my church to be a place where I encounter relational and programmatic opportunities to be engaged in my ongoing maturing—my growth into being my uniquely gifted self.

In designing your church's plan for providing growth opportunities, it is important to keep in mind three spiritual development priorities that arise out of a person-centered gift understanding.[10]

Three Priorities

First, a potential-filled journeyer must be aware of their need for ongoing formation and pursuing it. In Romans 12, the diversely gifted and mutually loving body is filled with people who are actively refusing to be conformed to the world; instead, they are actively seeking transformation.

Conformity, unless it is to Christ, is antithetical to being God's spectrum of grace in all its gifted diversity. Because our sinful natures pull us toward conformity, we all need transformation in order to be the unique expressions we each are on God's spectrum of grace.

We are always being formed one way or another. Conforming yields to the pressures to adopt a false self that tries to fit in this world. Yielding to God's transforming engages with your journey into your gifted true self, making the necessary sacrifices in the battles you must fight.

Paul wrote that there is something we must do to yield to God's transformative work in ourselves: present our bodies to him as living sacrifices. Repeated concrete and physical behaviors are required to experience God's transforming work. These are known as spiritual disciplines, and they are necessary for every potential-filled journeyer. Churches need to provide opportunities to learn spiritual disciplines.

Second, a potential-filled journeyer will learn to anchor their sense of security outside of this world's system. In chapter 7 we learned that Jesus and other mission-minded heroes anchored themselves through faith in what they'd heard from God and hope in the future God promised them. Faith and hope are learned character traits that deepen along the journey, growing stronger in life's battles.

God's Word fills in the content and focus for our faith and hope. The main focus provided is Jesus carrying his cross, living who he uniquely is.[11] Uniting that content and focus with relationships that witness to us an outside-this-world security (Hebrews 12:1) is powerful.

Peers and mentors are strategic for their inspiring examples and their belief in us—exhorting us that we, too, can learn to live on mission as our true selves. A church that encourages such relationships among people anchoring their security beyond this world's system is a powerful environment for growth.

Third, a person-centered understanding of spiritual gifts invites each of us to experience our lives as journeys in which we face up to enemies, increasingly growing into our unique identities and potentials. Chapters 2 and 6 introduce and apply Paul's idea of Israel's spoils journey as a metaphorical template for understanding our gifting journeys.

Understanding gift discovery and development as the spoils journey teaches us that as churches we must prioritize chronology, progress, and depth in supporting people's spiritual growth. By chronology I mean the potential-filled journeyers are able to locate themselves in their stories. Each one can look back and see the battles fought and spoils gained and look forward with a sense of those yet to be fought and gained. Then, as for progress, like the Israelites at their best, we are motivated to keep advancing into claiming more and more of God's inheritance for us. This sense of chronology and progress is realistic and strategic for our growth.[12]

Depth must also be prioritized. I previously mentioned that the turf on and for which we battle in the spoils journey is our hearts. The spoils metaphor teaches me that my journey involves reclaiming the parts of me that have been claimed and damaged by sin, a reclaiming that releases and energizes my potentials (gifts).

I need my church to point me to those heart battles, exposing my illusion that other people or circumstances are my real enemies, as well as the illusion that external behavioral change is sufficient. The heart is mentioned several hundred times in Scripture because that is where genuine transformation is needed and begins.

Layers of false beliefs and defense mechanisms, which constructed my false self, need to be penetrated and replaced by truth speaking in love. Real progress in my gifting journey will not happen through changes at superficial levels, but only by going to the necessary depth in my heart. I need my church to urge me to those depths.

Cultural Value: Maturing

In the Ephesians 4 gift passage, the only gifted people mentioned are those who lead. The emphasis is that they catalyze a body of maturing believers who help each other grow through their truth-in-love connections.

For a church to be a place where potential-filled journeyers find developmental support, they must experience that maturing is a cultural value there, modeled by the leaders. Specific programs and opportunities for growth should be offered, but their effectiveness will be tied to the extent to which maturing is an evident cultural value in the church.

Keeping in mind, then, the three spiritual development priorities that arise out of a person-centered gift understanding (see above), let's look at several specifics that display a church culture of maturing and offer entry points for journeyers.

First, our development requires us each to have a very small group of fellow journeyers who cultivate mutual transparency in trust. They are similar to me and my two friends mentioned in chapter 4, and Jaden's group with Rashad and Jon. In this inner circle, identification of each other's potentials and heart battles happens, and challenging truth in love is shared. Church leaders, model and encourage us to such inner circles! (More on this in chapter 10.)

Second, we each need the inspiration of mentors who have grown into their unique Christlike expression of their true selves. The primary value to me of my two mentors, Margaret and Robert, was their modeling of secure authenticity as they each ran after Jesus in their unique missions of serving. But they also explicitly provoked me to my own authenticity and unique mission. Christ-followers, look behind you for those you can inspire!

Third, at times our development can be encouraged by content-focused groups that study the Bible, another book, or go through a curriculum. A group study of this book would be an example. A study group is a task group and may include some relational connecting, though it cannot do what the purely relational inner circle does. Churches can offer group studies that are strategic for believers seeking transformation, security in God, and insights for their journeys.

Fourth, special events can be offered that provide training in spiritual, relational, and personal areas that support our development in community. Examples would be training in a) healthy listening skills to provide mutual support, b) spiritual disciplines to promote intimacy with Christ and transformation, and c) identifying our differing personality strengths and how we relate to one another. This last topic will be addressed further in chapter 16.

Fifth, since the battles I must fight are those of my heart, often I need a level of support in those battles that is deeper and more intense than a local church is equipped to provide. Churches cast their nets widely, inviting all to come to Christ. Thankfully, the body of Christ includes many parachurch ministries, such as workshops, seminars, and counseling. A local church wanting to support their potential-filled journeyers should form cooperative connections with parachurch opportunities.

In this chapter we've considered a church's support for people on their gifting journeys through teaching a perspective and encouraging personal growth. In the next chapter, we'll look at a church's support through fostering an *agape* environment and facilitating ministry involvement.

CHAPTER TEN

VALUES FOR CHURCH—FELLOWSHIP AND SERVICE

We looked at the ways churches can provide the cognitive and developmental support needed by potential-filled journeyers. We now turn to the ways a church can encourage journeyers by fostering a certain relational environment and facilitating their engagement with ministries.

FOSTERING THE *AGAPE* ENVIRONMENT

In chapter 4, we focused on the strategic role of powerful love for discovering and developing our giftedness. It is much more important to focus on love than on gifts, which is why Paul says the way of love is "more excellent" than the gifts (1 Corinthians 12:31). The person-centered, rather than gift-centered, understanding of gifts taught here is in sync with Paul's emphasis on love.

A church that helps its people develop deeper *agape* fellowship will be helping them in the discovery and development of their gifts. That is because in deeper *agape* people intersect with and accompany one another in their journeys of growth into their full potentials.

Intersection and accompaniment with one another at more vulnerable levels can lead to greater growth.

As implied in chapter 4, we need to be learners when it comes to loving sincerely and powerfully—we are not good at it by default. Our sinful self-centeredness is the problem, and it actively tries to deceive us into thinking how good we are at loving.

One of the main ways we deceive ourselves into thinking we're good at loving is by focusing on our external acts of service for others. While Scripture certainly charges us to love through concrete actions, it's interesting that in 1 Corinthians 13, in relation to gifts, Paul mentions that external actions of serving are sometimes not based in love (13:3). He then emphasizes that love involves deeper heart attitudes in our relationships with others (13:4–7).

It is those deeper *agape* attitudes in the heart that fashion how we connect and communicate with each other. This makes it possible to draw power from one another to face the battles in our journeys into our full potential. What is your church's strategy for helping people learn to love at the heart level? What is your plan for fostering *agape* environments for the potential-filled journeyers in your church?

Let's look at three aspects of a church strategy for this: providing a small group context, encouraging *agape* connections, and training in listening competencies.

Structural Context: Small Groups

Small groups have been an important phenomenon in local churches for some time now. Many helpful publications taught us that every Christian needs the strength that comes from being in a small group because that is where we practice the "one another's" of the New Testament.[1]

Group Qualities

Getting Christians to gather in small groups does not ensure those groups will connect at the levels that help them grow into their potentials. A church needs a clear target for the quality of the group fellowship for which it is aiming. I've mentioned before that qualities such as *agape* and listening are key. Broadly, there are two dimensions of small groups to keep in mind when developing your church's plan for groups: length and depth. But we can be more specific than that.

The context needed for walking alongside one another in our journeys is relationships of sufficient depth. A group's ability to develop such depth is affected by a) how long the group lasts, b) to what extent it includes a task (whether a study or some project), c) the size of the group, d) the makeup of the group (including marital status and gender), and e) what intentionality is applied to developing deeper relationships.

Here are some dynamics to consider in these areas:

- Since deeper relationships require getting to know one another well and developing trust, short-term groups rarely develop such depth. I suggest a minimum of six months of weekly meetings to develop such relationships. Shorter groups can be effective for other purposes.
- When a group adopts a task as part of its reason for being, that task requires group time, focus, and energy. Those requirements dilute the time, focus, and energy available for deeper relationships. The task might be studying the Bible or a book, an hour a week helping

a food pantry, etc. Task groups can serve important purposes, but their limits need to be remembered.
- The larger the group, the less able it is to connect at the necessary depth with everyone in the group. Keeping group size under ten is wise.
- Groups with diversity of marital status, gender, culture, age, and so on can be effective in building depth of connection, but they can also impose limitations on depth. Diversity of spiritual maturity is also a variable. There is no right or wrong plan, but leaders need to use wisdom to evaluate and guide diverse groups on a case-by-case basis.
- The words and actions of leaders clarify what level of intentionality about developing deeper relationships there will be in your church's groups.

Programmatically, we start fostering *agape* environments in church by creating the structural context of a small group ministry and encouraging believers to participate in those groups.

The groups in that structure should have the qualities we've just reviewed: a) no shorter than six months in length, b) making the relational connecting of potential-filled journeyers the top priority, c) nine or fewer group members, d) a workable mix of diversity and homogeneity, and e) leaders who are intentional about deepening group relationships.

Let's look further at the last quality just mentioned: intentional leaders.

Group Leaders

The group ministry structure must include trained leaders who are oriented to the journey dynamics of potential-filled people. If their orientation and training focuses leaders on the Journey View of gifting, they will possess clear intentionality when they lead a group. Leaders must be ready to guide people in integrating their spiritual growth with their spiritual gifting. Their learning of the themes in this book, and the behavioral areas emphasized here, such as listening and *agape*, are critical.

Your church's leadership core is strategic for inspiring group leaders to be oriented to supporting potential-filled journeyers, including creation of *agape* environments. In chapter 9, we noted that in Ephesians 4 only those with leadership gifts are mentioned. The picture is that they catalyze a body of believers who help each other grow through truth-in-*agape* connections.

Core leaders set a culture that values maturing in our journeys and the *agape* environments for doing so. They do this by speaking about these values and modeling participation in small groups practicing these values. Core leaders inspire and invite lay leaders into the strategically essential roles of being small group guides who intentionally foster *agape* environments for potential-filled journeyers.

The small group structural context for fostering *agape* environments includes intentional leaders who have received intentional training and orientation.

Group Types

While we're focusing on small groups, let's define a few kinds of groups that serve varying purposes. I mentioned some of these before and want you to have clarity about these group types. Other teachers have offered helpful categories and labels for understanding groups in churches. For purposes of this study, I'd like to clarify three group categories: inner circle, small group, and class.

Let's start with the one in the center of that list. We've looked at small group qualities and leaders in the last few pages. This type of group can form the centerpiece of your church's implementation of the Journey View. In those groups, we support one another in reflecting on our journeys, battles, and potentials.

A small group may be a hybrid of both a task and relational group, though the task elements must serve, or not interfere with, the relational priorities if it is to be a group supporting potential-filled journeyers.

So it may blend into its relational identity the task of studying the Journey View to orient participants to their gifting journeys. If the group lasts at least six months and gives significant time to connecting in each meeting, that can work well. Its characteristics often overlap with characteristics of the other two group types, and to be effective it should be no larger than nine people.

Then there is the inner circle, which is more intimate and more essential than the small group. I mentioned in chapter 9 the importance of having a very small group, which should be three or four close friends of the same sex. The inner circle is intentional at pursuing the transparency of each person and has no end date. The most significant experiences of truth-speaking in love happen there, and the most solid growth is spawned there.[2]

In small groups, people may develop friendships that can become inner circles, which might then replace the small group in meeting their needs for *agape* connection. That is an ideal outcome, and then those who are experiencing inner circles can sometimes serve as leaders for groups learning about *agape* connecting.

The third type of group I'll mention is classes. Often the popular view of gifts is applied in church through holding classes to teach people about spiritual gifts. In those classes, tests are usually given to help persons discern which gifts they have. The Journey View presents that, instead of classes and tests, it is relational small groups that are the context for gift discovery.

You and I need to be journeyers who are progressively reclaiming our potentials which have been damaged by sin. Taking a class and a test does not sufficiently address that need. Developing *agape* relationships of depth, in a small group and/or inner circle, can. These groups form the structural context for the power of *agape* to work. [3]

Experience: *Agape*

We previously (in chapter 4) looked intently at sincere love as the relational dynamic that Scripture connects with gifts and that provides power for us to discover and develop our potentials. Our earlier emphasis was that we need to give powerful *agape* to one another. Now we are looking at the environment that results when we give such love—our actual experiences when we are receiving powerful *agape*.

The Agape Evaluation (worksheet 1) clarifies love's specifics, from 1 Corinthians 13. Let's use one of those specifics to understand what your experience might be as you are being loved that way. Love "does not rejoice at wrongdoing, but rejoices with the truth" (13:6).

What will your experience be if I am loving you in a *13:6* way? You would be experiencing my sadness when I see you veering off the path of righteousness. And you would experience me enthusiastically cheering you on when I see you developing your potential-filled true self in whom Christ is being formed.

Relational experiences like that counter the world's pressure to conform rather than be transformed into who you uniquely are in Christ. If your small group consistently loves you with their authentic sadness and joy in a *13:6* way, you are powerfully invited to keep engaging with your battles and growing into your potentials! (Each of love's qualities on the Agape Evaluation can be applied from this vantage point of received experience.)

It is important for church leaders to be clear that these *agape* experiences are crucial for their people, and for small group ministry and group leaders to make these experiences the goal. They are where the rubber meets the road in terms of supporting potential-filled journeyers. And just as such *agape* is key to unlocking the potentials of individuals, its spread through a church's small groups can unlock a church's gifted potential corporately.

Skill: Listening

In chapter 8 we took an in-depth look at the strategic value of listening. Attentive listening is a concrete skill at the core of *agape* relating. It is also at the core of walking the gifting journey together because the scenes of gifting are within each of us. This listening dimension of love calls us to a deeper level of walking our journeys together, knowing one another's journeys more intimately.

As mentioned in chapter 8, there are many obstacles to becoming good listeners. The fact is that good listening is counter-cultural, whether the culture it counters is in society or the church. We also confront our own poor listening habits when we decide to learn listening.

Your church's small groups can be laboratories for learning and practicing healthy listening and seeing its loving impact on potential-filled journeyers. Yet our great lack in this area means we must intentionally provide training: people need knowledge and skills development. This is an area where classes are useful. Providing training classes in listening, coupled with small groups where people practice these skills, is an important implementation of the Journey View in your church.

I mentioned listening training in chapter 9 when we touched on special events to encourage personal growth. Here we see how it should be in tandem with relational groups where the taught skills are then practiced. I also mentioned that learning to be a listener is aided by deepening spirituality. That is another area where special events (e.g., training in the spiritual disciplines) can provide growth opportunities that enhance our mutual impact as fellow-journeyers in our small groups.

In the area of listening training, excellent resources are available. The curricula of Interpersonal Communication Programs have been most impactful for me.[4] But through an Internet search you can find numerous options for this important area of growth.

By this point in the book, you've realized that the Journey View of gifts involves a broader application in Christian life than the popular view. Now you can see that, as we integrate spiritual gifts with spiritual growth, we are also integrating the gifting journey with Christian fellowship. Learning loving listening helps us deepen the quality of our fellowship in the body of Christ.

FACILITATING MINISTRY INVOLVEMENT

Spiritual Gifts Reimagined does not emphasize categorization and ministry placement, which do tend to characterize the popular view of gifts. Instead, we have focused on each person's journey in developing their unique potential. While that is where the focus should be, it is also important to think about how we guide potential-filled journeyers into actual ministries.

Recruitment or Discipleship?

You'll remember my process with Jaden, which began when I met with him to talk about serving in youth ministry. Yet in getting to know him, I came to that fork in the road where I realized that if I only thought about getting him onto the ministry team, I'd have to pretend that the psychospiritual growth needs I saw weren't there.

I've made that mistake in pastoral ministry at times. It's a mistake with painful consequences, and it does not best serve people's needs. I encourage you to adopt a both/and approach that blends ministry recruitment with wise guidance about how someone's spiritual development status and needs relate to ministry service. Chapters 5–8 provide guidance for that both/and approach.

Categorizing for Ministry Matching

While it is more important to emphasize each person's gifted uniqueness, categorizing is still a useful tool, especially when it comes to narrowing down what kinds of ministries people best fit into. I'll say more about this topic in chapter 16, because the use of categorizing tools must be nuanced and has spiritual implications.

Here, I will simply say that such instruments can be useful whether they present categories of gifts or personalities or strengths, or other angles on how we humans differ from one another. They can assist a person in having the "sober judgment" about oneself that Paul relates to diverse giftedness in Romans 12:3. Insightful categorization ideally helps someone to value the unique person they are and use those strengths to bless others, not being envious of those with different gifts.

In the Journey View, we focus on people rather than gifts. Why? In part, because we interpret the scriptural gift list entries as categories of gifted people. These biblical categories are important for us for two reasons: they are inspired scripture, and they're designed for church application. In other words, they are telling us how the diversity of God's people is a match for the diverse needs of the body of Christ.

The Scriptures, then, are encouraging us to see categorization of people as a tool to understand how we meet the needs in the body of Christ. How will you encourage your church members to access the wisdom of categorization? And as they gain insight about themselves through categorizing instruments, how will you point them to ministry that matches their gifted potentials and serves the needs in your church?

Your church's plan for doing that will be unique to your situation, and I am not going to suggest any generic plan for how you should do it. But I am here commending the use of categorizing instruments, first in the service of helping people learn about their unique giftedness, and second to link people with fulfilling opportunities to serve others in the body of Christ.

The use of such cognitive education and testing should never overshadow the emphasis on the gifting journey we prioritize in this book. But categorization has its place, and in chapter 16 we will dig further into the use of categories, biblical and otherwise.

Spectrum Creativity

As we facilitate ministry involvement, we must remember that our goal is the discovery and unleashing of unique expressions of God's grace. Those discoveries of individuals combine to become the discovery of how your church is a unique corporate expression of God's grace. This is an organic, rather than an organizational, way to understand the dynamic of gifted persons making up the body of Christ.

The Journey View opens the door to seeing the creative hue each person is on God's spectrum of grace. Shifting our focus to potential-filled people, we notice the artist, the athlete, the accountant, the gardener, the organizer, the musician, and the mechanic as individual expressions of God's creative gifting.[5]

Yes, we can categorize them with biblical or other labels. But the wonder of God's grace is each gifted person. If you want to know what God wants to do in and through your church, you will set out to discover the unique individual expressions of his grace he has brought to your church. As you walk with them in their journeys of gifting, the spectrum of God's grace will shine brighter and brighter.

CHAPTER ELEVEN

ALL PEOPLE ARE GIFTED

When I married Susan, she owned a downtown coffee shop called The Artisan. Besides serving food and drink, it offered an intimate, laid-back venue for visual and performing arts. Though managed by Christians, artists and patrons of faith or non-faith used and loved The Artisan. It was a place of connection and culture, a space for celebrating the creativity of diverse people. A local newspaper once referred to it as "the living room" of our small city.

In every nook and cranny of our neighborhoods and communities there are gifted people. But what do spiritual gifts have to do with the unbelieving world?

The Journey View of spiritual gifts has elements within it that point us toward an awareness that our Creator has crafted every human being as uniquely gifted and invites everyone to discover and display their gifts during their journeys.

While some of the concepts that support using the idea of gifting beyond believers have been mentioned earlier in this book, they will be further discussed and developed in part 4. Nevertheless, here is the logical thought progression of the Journey View as it relates to unbelievers also being gifted:

1. In the Epistles, gifting is to be understood as metaphorical rather than concrete. New abilities are not added to believers.

2. The scriptural lists of gifts are category headings, each category filled with people, not gifts/abilities per se.

3. Thus gifting is not to be understood as simply functional, but referring to the diversity of whole persons God has created—whole persons born with their potentials/gifts.

4. This means that all persons are gifted and in need of growth to discover, develop, and use their potentials.

I am not suggesting that Paul and Peter were talking about unbelievers in their words about spiritual gifts. I am saying they were not teaching that believers have had new abilities added to them, and that points 1 and 2 above are accurate reflections of their thinking. I believe points 3 and 4 are reasonable understandings based on those scriptural interpretations.

The apostles' focus was on gifted believers in churches, but non-Christians, as humans created by God, have amazing and creative abilities. God just as lovingly and ingeniously designed and equipped my unbelieving friend as he did me. Sparks of God's beauty and wisdom are in everyone around us.

However, the most important event in the journey of gifting we've studied in this book is when a person receives God's Spirit at salvation, for the indwelling Spirit maximizes God's power, wisdom, and love for a person's development and use of their gifts. Someone who is not drawing from God's Spirit for their gift development can experience a variety of undesirable outcomes.

- They may have gifts that remain undiscovered or dormant.
- Development of their gifts may remain stunted.
- Gift use may be self-focused rather than other-focused.
- Praise for someone's gifts may be received for oneself rather than given to God.
- Gifts can be used in the service of ungodly or worthless efforts and goals.
- The very idea of being gifted can be twisted to promote ungodly values.

While these outcomes are possible in those who do not have God's Spirit living within, they can also occur in and through Christians who are not walking in step with the Holy Spirit. But a Christian who is walking her gifting journey in the Spirit's power can build a bridge to her unbelieving friend on the common ground that they're both gifted and needing growth to develop their gifting further.

At The Artisan, Christians and non-Christians together enjoyed God's spectrum of grace,[1] whether they thought of it that way or not. In our friendships and connections with unbelievers, there can be great value in noticing, delighting in, and encouraging their unique potentials. The vast array of gifts God has given extends beyond the arts to all kinds of strengths people have. *If being gifted with potentials is fundamental to being human, we can use this commonality to share the truth and love of Jesus.*

CONNECT AS JOURNEYERS

The Journey View invites us to give our attention to each person, regardless of spiritual status, as a creative expression of God's wisdom and to connect as fellow journeyers. This is an *agape* kind of connecting, and the features of *agape* we have looked at previously apply in these gospel-sharing relationships (chapters 4 and 8; also see worksheet 1).

Like you, your unbelieving friends were born with their gifted potentials. Also like you, they face the challenge of life's battles to discover, develop, and use those potentials. All kinds of obstacles lie in their paths and ours, from childhood through adulthood. We all share the need for encouragement and perspective to see the opportunities through the obstacles.

You probably know joyful stories of people growing into their potentials through life's trials, as well as sad stories of people not realizing and developing their unique gifts. The challenging journey of retrieving buried spoils is our common human ground. As noted in previous chapters, those battles are in people's hearts, where gifts may be layered over by life's wounds and the protective ways we learn to avoid more wounding.

This means that shared understanding and shared strength is a real possibility across lines of faith and non-faith. And there can be shared joy, because when I glimpse the unique giftedness of my unsaved friend, am I not seeing the creativity of my God? And this sharing of understanding, strength, and joy is a two-way street since we are both needing to navigate this common human journey.

In this kind of gospel-connecting, using skills of active listening is strategic. That is because a) you are on a quest to discover the unique person before you, so you must be genuinely attentive, and b) the gift you give of helping someone feel heard will be impactful for their gift development. We looked earlier (see chapters 8 and 10) at how *agape* is communicated powerfully through listening.

Notice how this basic connecting is similar whether it's with a Christian or a non-Christian, because of our common needs. The Journey View invites us to affirm the gifts of unbelievers, and to come alongside them in our common journey. Of course, as I mentioned, the disadvantage the unbeliever has is that she or he lacks the indwelling Holy Spirit to empower their gift development. But our connecting can point them in that direction.

POINT TO CHRIST

The Source of Our Gifting

As I connect with my unbelieving friend in ways that affirm his gifts, I am also sharing my own story about my gifts and their development. It's an opportunity to model gratitude for my gifts, and to make it clear that my gratitude is to God. My witness is that I see him as the One who has blessed me with my gifts. I also thank and praise God for my non-Christian friend's gifts, and can display those attitudes to him.

I've implied in earlier chapters, and will explain more explicitly in part 4, that the Journey View of gifts is Christocentric rather than Spirit-centered. We saw that Paul points to Christ as the gift-giver in Ephesians 4:7–10. In the context of sharing the good news of Christ with others, it makes sense to point to Jesus as the One who gets the credit for the gifts we have received.

Cross-Carrying

In chapter 7 we learned that cross wisdom leads us to see how Jesus carrying his cross is a model for our own gift development and expression. His call to follow him by taking up our own crosses

(Mark 8:34) includes a call to uniqueness amid community, diversity within unity.

We also saw that Jesus' cross-carrying was his unique servanthood mission. In carrying your cross, you are not only identifying your uniqueness, you are expressing it in a servanthood mission. This is often quite different from the world's way of telling you to express your identity. In the world's system, self-fulfillment and self-expression are ends in themselves. In Scripture, servanthood that furthers God's kingdom is the outflow of your identity development.

In such servanthood, you experience fulfillment as you learn and express how you uniquely follow our cross-carrying Christ. Christians are each called to channel their unique package of potentials into service to others. You can tell unbelievers that you serve in the unique ways you are gifted because that is what following Christ involves. This can be a witness to them that Jesus also delights in their unique potential to serve others. Following Jesus is the path to such fulfillment.

This witness invites people to reconsider what they've thought about Jesus, and to consider three dynamics his example presents to them. The first is that it's normal to face opposition as you develop and express your uniqueness. Jesus faced those challenges as he carried his cross, and we should expect to. This forms another point of commonality between believer and unbeliever because all people can face opposition, even before they're Christ-followers.

The second dynamic also presents opportunity for connecting and for pointing to Christ: the battle between the true self and false self, which we considered in chapter 7. This struggle, largely set up by the first dynamic, pressures us toward imitation of others and suppression of our unique gifting. Jesus expressed his unique true self as he lived in faithfulness to the cross mission that flowed out of that identity.

It is human to want to be accepted by others, setting up a false self for that reason. We can all benefit from friends who will point out to us when we are sacrificing our own unique potential in order to fit in with the crowd. The witness to unbelievers that Jesus is the model for fidelity to their true selves encourages further discussions about what it means to follow him and why to follow him.

I suggested the third dynamic earlier when I highlighted that Jesus' expression of his unique identity and mission was in the form of servanthood. Both believers and unbelievers will find themselves detouring into a focus on self, rather than finding ultimate fulfillment in using one's unique potentials to serve God and others. Unbelievers often discern that serving others is more fulfilling than serving self. We can point to Jesus as the example of this wisdom.

In following the command to "go . . . and make disciples" (Matthew 28:19), believers are challenged to invite unbelievers to also respond to the God who has created each unique person and to Jesus who calls us to the journey of growing in that uniqueness. We can meet them on the common ground of being gifted creations of God who face the opportunities and challenges that presents. We can point them to the Lord and Savior, and to the atoning power of his unique cross mission.

Body of Christ

If we are pointing to the inspiration of Christ for the journey of developing gifted uniqueness, we must accompany that with the display of loving unity in his body. If I'm inviting my unbelieving friend to join me in following Jesus, then he needs to see Christians giving journey support to one another in the church. It needs to be evident that the *agape* relating we've discussed in previous chapters is real in Christ's body.

For as we are pointing to Jesus we must be pointing to his body on earth. We've seen in the gift passages in Romans, 1 Corinthians, and Ephesians that the environment for sharing our gifted variety with one another is love. It's true in Peter's words about gifts too: "Above all, keep loving one another earnestly. . . . As each one has received a gift, use it to serve one another, as good stewards of God's varied grace" (1 Peter 4:8, 10).

The invitation to follow Jesus on the journey of gift discovery, development, and use should also be an invitation to join such a loving community.

DEALING WITH THE DIVERSITY ISSUE

Popular view presentations about gifts do not usually comment on how spiritual gift diversity relates to the diversity that is discussed and debated in our society today. That is because the popular view sees gifts as new abilities added to Christians only. Therefore, it is a specialized topic relevant for churches, not broader society.

The Journey View, as mentioned before and explained in part 4, sees gifting as metaphorical and the gift lists as people categories. In presenting this metaphor (and others) and categorizing people, the apostles were responding to the diversity of people they saw in the body of Christ, seeking to build unity. Churches dealt with a diversity of people in the first century, and still do today. The Journey View focuses on diverse whole persons born with their potentials, rather than on diverse added gifts.

Our society is seeking to embrace diversity. Understanding spiritual gifts is part of God's wisdom for responding to diversity. Even though the diversity addressed through spiritual gift wisdom in Scripture is different than the diversity the world is pursuing, *there are aspects of gift wisdom, especially from a Journey View perspective, that can form part of a Christian witness to our world as it pursues diversity.*

Contrast with the World

Since the goal of this chapter is that we use our common ground of being gifted humans for gospel witness, let's look briefly at how that witness can display a contrast to the world's ways of pursuing diversity.

- First, instead of focusing on people as instances of this or that category, we are interested in each individual as a unique expression of God's wisdom.
- Second, instead of pursuing power to establish the validity of someone's category, we relate in *agape* ways and use listening to communicate the value God gives to each individual.
- Third, instead of asserting pride and rights to feel valued, we experience value in God's grace gifting of each of us and rest in humility.
- Fourth, instead of elevating some classes of people over others, we affirm the equally wonderful gifting of each person.
- Fifth, instead of trusting evolving human authorities on human diversity, we trust our Creator's revealed scriptural wisdom as the truth about our diversity.

- Sixth, instead of pretending that sin doesn't corrupt human understandings and our embrace of diversity, we acknowledge that our sin inclines all of us to rebel against God's wisdom about our diversity.
- Lastly, instead of pursuing the disappointing mirage of "just being myself," we pursue the eternal horizon of each becoming fully and uniquely ourselves as we become fully like Christ.

These God-oriented postures become part of our gospel witness to each gifted unbeliever. They form a contrast to the false gospel of the world.

Part of the reason the Journey View of spiritual gifts has something to say to society that is pursuing diversity in its worldly way is that this view of gifts does not separate task from being. The popular view does, teaching that being gifted is only about what we do, not who we are.[2]

The Journey View presents that we each have a unique identity and out of that flows our unique lives of gifted service to God and others. We saw in chapter 7 how that mission-oriented way of living is our response to Christ's call to follow him. In worldly diversity, people are seeking to find their identity without the context of the truth that is in Christ. But when I understand that my unique gifting by Christ reflects my unique identity in Christ, the truth that is in Christ guides my search for identity.

It is beyond the scope of this book to explore further how worldly diversity differs from the diversity that sprang from God's heart in his creation of the human race. Worldly diversity is a perversion of the godly diversity that grace-gifts display. But as Christians relate in love to diverse gifted unbelievers, our reflection of God's delight in each unique person can be a witness to the good news of Christ.

God's Spectrum

In chapter 1 we considered the illustration of grace as a prism. The world's rainbow illustration seems to invite us to worship diversity, rather than its Artist.[3] Based on Peter's and Paul's use of the word *poikilos* to teach us about how we display God's variegated creativity, I proposed to you that God's grace and wisdom are like a prism that refracts his creativity into the spectrum that we are (1 Peter 4:10; Ephesians 3:10).

Our focus must be on the prism and the One whose creative expressions are refracted through his grace and wisdom. The Maker of all this variety is holy and lifted up, exalted above the heavens. The Giver of diverse spiritual gifts is the ascended Christ, who is "far above . . . every name that is named, not only in this age but also in the one to come" (Ephesians 1:21; cf. 4:7–8).

Our world's attempts to describe diversity fall far short of the truth, grace, and wisdom of God. Learning through Scripture about his love and holiness, and about his responses to our sinfulness in his truth and grace, is essential to get an accurate understanding of the human diversity he has created.

If my delight in each unique person on God's spectrum of grace is united with my awe of the spectrum's Artist, I can point people to the God whose character shapes that diversity.

PART FOUR

STUDY THE CONCEPTS

Part 4 goes behind the scenes of the Journey View. In chapters 13 through 15, we will focus on how Scripture supports this interpretation of spiritual gifts. Before diving into that, we will briefly survey three options for a view on gifts in chapter 12.

Since our natural reaction to the diversity of people is to categorize, and since discovering the uniqueness of each person is a value in the Journey View, chapter 16 will explore the tension between categorization and uniqueness.

Finally, chapter 17 deals with gifts that are supernatural in their character, seeking to understand how they fit in a Journey View perspective on spiritual gifts.

CHAPTER TWELVE

THREE VIEWS ON GIFTS

The doctrine of spiritual gifts deserves a second look. When Christians, including authors and Bible teachers, have focused on spiritual gifts, they direct most of their attention to either the definition and use of each gift in church life, or to the debated points between charismatics and noncharismatics.

Those debates often generate a lot of passion on both sides as we emphasize the big differences between them. And there are varying views of the subject within each camp. All this makes for a lot of attention being sucked up. But perhaps missed in those debates is that those two camps share a fundamental operating assumption about spiritual gifts.

The shared operating assumption widespread among Christians of many diverse denominations and convictions is that the scriptures about gifts should be interpreted to mean that God adds to believers special gifts when they each receive the Spirit. (Some say that happens at salvation; some say it is later.) They agree that those special gifts are new abilities, whether temporary or permanent. It is also usually agreed that those new abilities are different than one's natural talents.

This popular view needs a second look. Is it a solid biblical interpretation? Are there other reasonable ways to interpret the scriptures about gifts?[1]

The topic of spiritual gifts got little attention through the centuries since the New Testament was written. When it began to get more attention in the twentieth century, a lot of the focus was on the supernatural gifts. Once a broader focus on all the gifts began around the 1970s, with the aim of empowering laity for ministry, the view that spiritual gifts are added-on abilities spread in popularity.

Until recently, I was not aware of any published works that took exception with the popular view. While working on this book, which is based on my 1998 Doctor of Ministry final project, I came across Kenneth Berding's 2006 book, *What Are Spiritual Gifts? Rethinking the Conventional View*.[2]

The question in Berding's title goes to the heart of the issue: What are spiritual gifts? Are they indeed added-on abilities? Above I indicated that most Christians assume the answer to that question is yes. It may be difficult to even notice that the question "what are spiritual gifts?" is not asking for a list of gifts or a definition of each gift but asking a broader and more foundational question.

In answering that question, Berding and I both teach that Scripture does *not* indicate that spiritual gifts are added abilities. As we each go on to define what gifts are, however, we have different answers and emphases. I find Berding's book very helpful as a detailed critique of the traditional view's interpretation of Scripture. We both underline the belief that the doctrine of spiritual gifts needs a second look.

To help you further consider what your answer to the question, "What are spiritual gifts?" will be, I will now briefly summarize my understanding of three differing options for answering that question: the Mechanical (traditional or popular) View, the Minimalist (Berding's ministries) View, and the Metaphorical (Journey) View presented in this book. These three titles are, of course, my characterizations of those views.

In my brief summaries of the Mechanical and Minimalist views my intent is not to major on critique or provide refutations. My purpose is to clarify those as distinct options for a doctrine of spiritual gifts, but I do so from the Journey View perspective. Likewise, this chapter's summary of the Metaphorical View is not intended as an argument for it (that is spread throughout this book) but as a clarification of how it contrasts with the other two views.

THE MECHANICAL (POPULAR) VIEW

Describing this view is challenging, since it is the popular view and is therefore represented by many teachers and publications, both charismatic and noncharismatic. Though it has many variations in detail and emphasis, and conflicting convictions, there are commonalities. *In grouping all these variations together as "the Mechanical View," I am focusing on their belief in the automatic addition of new abilities to whole persons in the midst of their developmental journeys.*[3]

The role of the Holy Spirit in gift-giving has a prominent place in the popular view. While the Spirit is not mentioned in direct association with gift-giving in Romans, Ephesians, and 1 Peter, he is repeatedly mentioned in the first part (12:1–13) of the 1 Corinthians gifts passage. Paul refers to the Spirit only minimally in the rest of his extended discussion of gifts in that Epistle (12:14–14:40).

The popular view usually derives a mechanical understanding of gift-giving from those mentions of the Spirit, by linking the Spirit's distribution of gifts (12:11) with the Spirit's baptism of believers (12:13), though that link is not explicit in the text.

So whether the popular view proponent sees Spirit baptism as happening at salvation, or happening later, gift-receiving becomes a point-in-time automatic event that is likely unknown to (or unanticipated by) the believer at the time.[4] I use the terms "mechanical" and "automatic" for this view because in it gifting seems detached from a person's developmental status (e.g., spiritual maturity level) and from their identity uniqueness (e.g., personality), and appears to involve the following:

- The gift lists are made up of various added-on abilities; that is, a spiritual gift is something you get.
- Unlike other personal abilities, development of your new abilities (gifts) is not emphasized.
- What is often prioritized instead is taking a test to discover your new abilities.
- The point of your spiritual gifts is their uses or functions; they are utilitarian.
- You are divided into a spiritual part and a natural part; your spiritual gifts are different than your natural talents (sacred versus secular).
- We are directed to learn what each gift is and does instead of learning about one another as unique expressions of God's grace.

Perhaps you will point out that these are generalizations that do not apply in all situations, which I readily and gratefully acknowledge.

However, churches that give any emphasis to spiritual gifts tend to reflect these generalizations by doing some of the following:

- They stress cognitive education about gifts more than how personal growth affects gift discovery and use.
- For identification of gifting, they stress use of a testing instrument over feedback in long-term relationships.
- More value is placed on successful categorization of people than on God's unique creativity seen in each individual.
- There is emphasis on placement within existing roles more than on the Spirit's ongoing shaping of each church as he adds and develops unique persons.
- In churches that welcome miraculous gift expressions, amazement at those may lead to overlooking the journey of gifting each believer must walk.

The reality of spiritual gifting calls us to deeper ministry with persons than what we traditionally do within this utilitarian understanding of gifts. A mechanistic understanding of gifting overlooks the real battles we each must fight to discover and develop our gifts.

THE MINIMALIST (MINISTRIES) VIEW

Kenneth Berding is a New Testament professor at an evangelical seminary, and his critique of the popular view (in *What Are Spiritual Gifts?*) is not that it is mechanical but that it is not true to Scripture.[5] He demonstrates that an emphasis on believers' abilities is foreign to the apostle Paul's writings, including the gift passages.[6] Instead, he argues, Paul's consistent emphasis is on ministry roles and functions, and every believer is assigned by God to specific ministries.

Berding believes that the phrase "spiritual gift" corrupts our understanding of Scripture's teaching on the subject, as the connotations associated with "gift" in English are different than its meaning in New Testament Greek. Especially confusing, he writes, is the English usage of the word to denote special talents certain people have, which, he says, is foreign to its use in the New Testament.[7] He demonstrates that *charisma* is not used to denote abilities but covers a broader range of ideas.[8]

Berding's view is that Paul's main focus in giving us the "so-called" gift lists,[9] and in teaching the metaphor of the church as a body, is to promote the healthy functioning and building up of the local church.[10] The lists, he teaches, are not actually gift lists, but ministry lists.[11] The application intended is for every believer to be actively involved and serving in ministry. Spending time in trying to discover one's gifts is "unnecessary and even unhelpful."[12]

While Berding's book and this book both present that spiritual gifts are not added abilities, he provides a detailed in-depth argument that this book does not: an extensive analysis of Scripture passages and words that undermines the gifts-as-abilities view. He also teaches that Bible translations often write the popular view into various verses and passages, misleading their readers.[13] If you follow my suggestion and take a second look at spiritual gifts, I recommend that you study Berding.

Another touch point between *What Are Spiritual Gifts?* and this book concerns the identification of what the list entries are. I have said they are not entities you receive but rather category headings. Berding speaks of the list entries as "representative."[14] We both move away from the idea that the list entries are entities or abilities and see them as chosen with a view to application to local churches.

However, we disagree about what is being represented or categorized. He sees the content as focusing on the diverse activities that strengthen the church: ministries, roles, functions, assignments. I see the content as focusing on the diverse spectrum of people God has created, with the category groupings and headings chosen to highlight application to church.

I believe groups of people united in love is the main vision in these passages, while Berding emphasizes healthy functioning that strengthens churches.[15]

Berding's view appropriately challenges every Christian to be actively serving in the body of Christ. But as he exposes the mistaken interpretation that people receive new abilities at salvation, he directs our attention away from people and toward tasks. He minimizes the reality of a diversity of gifted people, teaching that Paul is simply saying to find a ministry role and serve.

Berding's verdict on gifting language is that it is problematic and should not be used.[16] I believe it is appropriate but should be understood metaphorically. Berding believes the canonical connections of the gift passages focus us on ministry roles.[17] I believe they focus us on the journey of gifting. In guiding us to avoid the errors of the popular view, I believe Berding takes us in a minimalist direction. In contrast, I believe the metaphors associated with spiritual gifts in Scripture expand our understanding.

FILLING THE VACUUM

It is not surprising that there have been significant disagreements about spiritual gifts for many years, particularly between charismatics and noncharismatics. Nor is it surprising that it is possible on these pages to clarify three very different approaches to what gifts are about—all claiming to be biblical, even when we set aside the more attention-getting disagreements.

Why are there so many differing ideas about spiritual gifts? One reason is the amount and type of information about gifts in the Bible. The major doctrines of the Christian faith command large portions of Scripture, often with extensive detail and development. Relative to those doctrines, the topic of spiritual gifts dominates very few pages of the New Testament. And the emphasis of those pages is practical application, not precise doctrinal definition.

God has put in Scripture what he wants us to know about spiritual gifts. But because the explicit passages about gifts are limited in size and styled for application, Bible teachers have their work cut out for them in helping Christians understand what spiritual gifts are—filling the vacuum in our understanding of gifts. That vacuum needs to be filled with discerning how spiritual gifts fit in the matrix of biblical revelation.

The popular view seems to settle for what the gift passages *appear* to be saying and fills our vacuum of understanding with the thinking that gifts are new abilities added to us. I believe that view has largely neglected the work of integrating spiritual gifts with other scriptures. Berding works hard to contextualize spiritual gifts within New Testament revelation, particularly Paul's letters, resulting in his spiritual ministries view.

The view presented here is that the spiritual gift passages are snapshots of a broader scriptural panorama of people developing and displaying their diverse potentials, and that those passages and their contexts contain clues that lead us into that panorama.

THE METAPHORICAL (JOURNEY) VIEW

In the Metaphorical View, the apostles' burden in the scriptures about gifts has to do with people rather than abilities or roles.

Most of our thinking about gifts is shaped by Paul's writings, and he is addressing the priority of unity amid diversity, a unity that requires love. He tells us that our identity together is the body of Christ. Peter's burden is also about people, but his mention of gifts prioritizes serving one another. He tells us this is important because our identity together is as an alien witness in this world: a spiritual house (1 Peter 2:5).

Paul and Peter believe that Christians in churches need to imagine what life together is supposed to look like. They employ metaphor to powerfully drive home to churches how we are to see ourselves: a body and its members, a spiritual house and its royal priesthood. They exhort us to specific attitudes toward one another as we turn these images into relational reality.

As they introduce gifting language to continue to press their cases for unity and mutual service, they do not stop using metaphor. Paul and Peter present the powerful image that we are each grace-gifted. They will not allow us to see some as wonderfully gifted and others as average or also there. The metaphor of grace-gifting teaches us how to perceive one another. Our community is full of unique expressions of God's grace! We are each wonderfully gifted!

- Thus, instead of focusing on abilities or roles, we focus on knowing each other. We cultivate relationships of powerful love in which we value and nurture each other as grace-expressions.

- Instead of focusing on utilitarian abilities that fit into roles, we find our breath taken away by beauty: the metaphor of the variegated spectrum of God's grace that we are.
- Instead of isolating gifting as something different than life's real challenges and opportunities, we are drawn through metaphor into the journey of retrieving our spoils as we engage the necessary battles.
- Instead of treating the gift list entries as things we get, we understand them as categories of people.
- Instead of focusing on which category we're each in, Christ carrying his cross becomes metaphor for our lives: united in following him, each identifying our diverse crosses.

Spiritual gifts are a window to these powerful realities. We see through that window to these realities when we integrate the topic of gifts with its connected scriptural themes. I am not saying that Paul's and Peter's specific verses about gifts include or explain all these connected themes. I am saying that their teachings about gifts contain threads to these themes and with them form a biblical perspective on spiritual gifts.

I have developed in this book the clues in the gifts texts that link to these themes and will discuss them further in subsequent pages. The metaphor of spiritual gifting, along with the further metaphors in these canonical connections, make up the powerful metaphorical understanding (Journey View) of spiritual gifts.

CHAPTER THIRTEEN

INTERPRETIVE FACTORS

APOSTOLIC PERSPECTIVE

Occasion and Theology

Our scriptural sources for direct teaching on spiritual gifts are four New Testament Epistles, three written by the apostle Paul, and one written by the apostle Peter. They are all written to churches, but each letter has distinctive characteristics that form its context for introducing the topic of spiritual gifts. The author fashioned each letter to address or respond to the needs he was aware of in its recipients. Bible scholars say that each Epistle has its particular "occasion."[1]

It's important to keep that in mind when we study the topic of gifts in these Epistles. We tend to approach these studies with the desire to find a clearly defined doctrine about spiritual gifts. We want to easily move from the verses we read in the explicit spiritual gift passages to a finished understanding about gifts that we can believe and teach.

But if we do that, we risk violating a fundamental guideline about how to use Scripture to build our systematic theology. Osborne states it this way:

We dare not read individual statements [of Scripture] as finished dogma but rather must move from the individual statements to ascertain the biblical theology and then to develop a dogmatic or systematic theology.[2]

When Paul and Peter wrote about gifts in their letters, they were not trying to say all there is to say about spiritual gifts. Instead of trying to write a theology of spiritual gifts, they were communicating what they felt those readers needed to learn, given what each apostle knew about their circumstances.

Let's take Paul's teachings on gifts in 1 Corinthians as an example. If we're doing careful biblical study, we'll start our studies of gifts in that Epistle by developing an understanding of the whole letter, how the sections on gifts fit into the whole letter, and what situations of the Corinthians Paul is addressing.

That will give to us part of what I am calling the apostolic perspective in 1 Corinthians, which affects what Paul chooses to say and emphasize about gifts in that letter. But that study of 1 Corinthians would not give to us a systematic theology of spiritual gifts. It would just be one building block of that.

In general, the popular view has given us aspects of a systematic theology (Osborne's "finished dogma") of gifts based on some of the individual statements of 1 Corinthians 12. For example, we are told that the Spirit literally distributes gifts to each Christian when they are baptized in the Spirit, based especially on 12:11, 13. If that interpretation occurred to you in your study, it would be better to jot it down as a possibility, but hold it as tentative until you'd finished the rest of your scriptural studies about gifts.

The occasions of these letters color what is included in them about gifts, and how it is presented. The apostles were not trying to present a complete and systematic theology of gifts. Instead, it is left for us to study the scriptures about gifts and follow their canonical connections (discussed further below). In that way we can build a biblical theology about gifts, which I attempt to do in this book, with emphasis on life application.

It's also the case that the appearance of the gift lists in letters that are "occasional" should affect how we understand what the lists are.

Gift Lists: Observation and Variation

Paul and Peter each have their apostolic perspective as they write to various groups, and Paul's perspectives vary somewhat from letter to letter. This is one reason why Paul's lists of gifts vary each time he presents them. With each different list, the apostle is saying to those people "here's what I think you need to know" or "here's what relates to your situation." And the writers' judgments about that are a little different in each letter.

I used to assume there is a "correct list of spiritual gifts," and that maybe one day someone would win that debate and we could all stop arguing! But when, in a seminary class forty years ago, a professor reminded me that the biblical authors (in general) didn't have the words of Scripture dictated to them, a light bulb went on inside me about these lists.

I looked in vain in the texts for any indication that Paul or Peter received special revelation about what the gifts are. As I concluded that these two apostles made up their own lists, I began the process of interpreting their words in the contexts of each Epistle. This was just the beginning of discerning a different doctrine of spiritual gifts.

A key point in my study was determining that, in coming to their lists, Paul and Peter were looking at people—diverse groups of people. In other words, they came up with categories of people. First, they observed, and second, they categorized what they observed. In this view, then, the lists are not based in direct revelation, but in observation. Their observations are overlapping from list to list, but subject to variation.

The Gift Lists: Individuals or Churches?

What is important about that conclusion is that the lists are not about things we get called gifts, but rather about people. In our understanding and application of scripture concerning gifts, then, we should be focusing on people rather than on gifts as entities. Paul and Peter came up with categories of people, so the list entries are headings for people categories. Focusing on people, therefore, is what we have done in this book. The Journey View is person-centered rather than gift-centered.

This does not mean that the apostles' categorizations are unimportant. The categorizations are inspired scripture. Yet the several different category lists, all inspired, are flexible, adjusted to fit the occasion of each letter. This in itself suggests that the lists are based in apostolic perception and observation, fluctuating with the circumstances.

Anytime we categorize, we do so from a particular perspective, based on our current perceptions. I will say more about categorization in chapter 16, but the general perspective of Paul and Peter when they categorized gifted people was church application. When they devised their category headings, they were thinking about how diverse people serve in local churches. Categorization of people can be done from many perspectives, but healthy church functioning is their angle.

Thus, the normative importance of these lists for us has to do with understanding how diverse congregations of people mutually serve together to produce healthy churches.

In that view, the lists are saying more about churches than about individual people. A book on church health might use these lists as a biblical grid for describing a well-functioning congregation. In contrast, this book focuses on the gifting of individuals. To understand how individuals become gifted, we should use a panoramic lens to discern a biblical theology of gifting rather than a microscope to examine only the lists and the immediate verses around the lists.

The Journey View of Gifts

In the gift passages of the Epistles, Paul and Peter do not explicitly develop a journey understanding of gifting for individuals. They instead focus on church health in various ways. But there are implications in their contexts (especially concerning spiritual growth), and clues left—biblical threads to follow—that help us fill out our understanding of individual gifting. We have followed those threads in this book.[3]

The popular view of gifts has usually zeroed in on the lists themselves, taking these category headings and making them into abilities people get that relate to serving in diverse ways. Though wise use of categories can be helpful for individuals, that view has emphasized individual application from lists that are more about congregational application. The scenes of individual gifting are not to be found in those lists but in their contexts and canonical connections.

Study of these broader biblical connections, I believe, leads to the Journey View of gifting. To further understand the interpretive path that leads to this conclusion, we need to say more about the apostles' use of metaphor, making canonical connections, and integration with spiritual growth.

USE OF METAPHOR

Grace-Source

If the apostles did not receive direct revelation of lists of gifts that are given at Spirit baptism, then the giving and receiving of gifts should not be understood in a mechanical or automatic way. The popular view makes the error of reifying gifts and gift-giving. To reify something means "to consider or represent (something abstract) as a material or concrete thing: to give definite content and form to (a concept or idea)."[4]

Alongside the metaphor of the body Paul lays the metaphor of gifting, all in the service of God's people seeing what unity in diversity looks like in Christ. He introduces the concept of *charismata*, directing people toward grace as the source of our diverse potentials. It is that truth about the grace-source of all of our strengths that is the learning point of the metaphor for us.

Osborne points out that an ancient metaphor "overlapped" with the reality it signified "only at one point," and that modern interpreters may force a biblical metaphor to indicate several ideas about the reality it's signifying.[5]

This mistake can create doctrine about a biblical topic that is not intended by the biblical text, such as the teaching that gifts are new abilities we get from the Spirit at conversion. That view is a reification of the metaphor of gifting. Theologian Don Payne sees "Thomistic underpinnings" behind this reification.[6]

The one overlapping point of the metaphor is grace-source, thus the term *charismata*. Osborne further points out that it is how the metaphorical image is dissimilar to the readers' default perceptions that leads them to "rethink" their perspective.[7] Paul's Corinthian readers were impressed by *pneumatika*. Through the *charismata* metaphor, Paul says let's shift our focus to grace-source for all kinds of gifts.

Metaphorical impact

As Paul and Peter addressed the needs in congregations, they used the metaphor of gifting as part of their apostolic guidance. We are to see each other as whole persons who are grace-expressions. Understanding gifting as a metaphor and the lists as people categories means that we should not be looking for spiritual gifts that are abilities distinct from our natural talents.

The potentials we have for good, as unique individuals on God's spectrum of grace, are all sourced in God and his grace. I mentioned above Dr. Don Payne's concern about Thomism's impact on our doctrine of spiritual gifts. He also sees that philosophy's "dichotomy of 'natural' and 'supernatural'" as influencing this area, "resulting in the assumption that spiritual gifts are unrelated to 'natural' abilities (as if there are any abilities that are not from God)."[8]

There is no need to say that a wonderful musical ability is a natural talent that can express the spiritual gift of encouragement. Or that the ability to counsel others is a natural talent that uses the spiritual gift of wisdom. Or that the skills used by a surgeon, landscaper, bus driver, or athlete are in the natural, not the spiritual, arena.

While at one level these perspectives do no harm, I believe they are based on a faulty reified interpretation and distract us from focus on each unique person's important gifting journey. And the theological dichotomy is suspect, which may fail to appreciate how God is glorified by the totality of a person's potential.

Seeing gifting as a metaphor clarifies this wholeness of human persons, and the Journey View sees layer upon layer of metaphor: body of Christ, gifts and gifting, spectrum of grace and wisdom, gifts as spoils, carrying your cross as expression of unique mission based on your gifting.[9]

Scripture invites us, therefore, to follow its imaginative expansion of gifting through these layers of metaphor.[10] As we've seen in earlier chapters, this has impact for us as individual journeyers, as believers together, and as witnesses to those not yet in the body of Christ.

CANONICAL CONNECTIONS

No one human writer of Scripture sets out a full understanding of spiritual gifting. And piecing together the information in only the explicit gift passages has resulted in a Mechanical View of gifting which is unrelated to spiritual growth and often to the important role of loving community for gift development.

In chapter 12 I referred to our vacuum of understanding about gifts, saying it is due to the fact that the explicit biblical teachings about gifts are a) limited in amount, and b) styled for application rather than clear doctrinal definition. I believe it is not possible to construct a complete understanding of spiritual gifting just on the passages that explicitly talk about gifts. The theme of gifts needs to be integrated with other relevant biblical themes, especially concerning spiritual development.

The first step in that integration is to study the gift passages in their contexts. For example, we've mentioned how, in Romans 12, personal transforming and proper self-perception flow into diverse gifting. That's an example of the importance of immediate context. In 1 Corinthians we've seen that Paul's doctrine of the body and gifts in chapter 12 is to be viewed through the lens of the cross, which is the apostle's emphasis back in his chapter 1. That's a step beyond immediate context.

In Ephesians 4 the challenge to contextualize the scriptures about gifts gets a major shove that goes beyond that letter and even beyond the New Testament. Paul directs our attention to Psalm 68, which becomes a window to the spoils motif that stretches from Genesis to the Minor Prophets. I believe Paul is saying that gifting has been seen before, and have set forth the implications for our spiritual journeys (chapter 2).

The topic of spiritual gifts is not a stand-alone doctrine. It needs this integration to be fully understood. Biblical threads from the explicit gift passages lead us to these immediate and more distant scriptures. On the topic of gifts, we are connecting the dots within the canon of Scripture that will draw for us a fuller picture of spiritual gifting. And something amazing happens as that picture emerges: it draws our focus to Jesus Christ.

In our reimagining of gifts, we've been drawn to focus on the cross of Jesus and his victorious ascension. According to D. A. Carson, scriptural exposition at its best draws attention to the "canonical connections that inexorably move toward Jesus Christ."[11] I believe the Journey View of gifts does just that.

GIFTS AND GROWTH[12]

Some popular view publications about gifts include acknowledgement of the importance of spiritual maturing for gift development and use. Many do not. In the Journey View, we cannot speak of spiritual gifting without speaking of spiritual growth. I mentioned in the preface my pastoral frustrations with recruiting gifted people without regard for their needs for further growth. The story of Jaden in part 2 is intended to illustrate the integration of gifting with growth in a ministry setting.

The theme of spiritual growth seems explicit or implicit in varying ways in every New Testament Epistle. Indeed, all of Scripture provides "training" in righteous living (2 Timothy 3:16). Spiritual growth can be studied and pursued in multiple dimensions:

- growth in holiness
- strengthening of faith
- knowing and emulating Christ
- living in God's presence
- growing in love and grace
- deepening in God's Word
- maturing in wisdom
- authentic Christian fellowship
- gospel connections with unbelievers

All these areas and more are areas for Christian growth, development, progress, or journey. Each is a facet of becoming mature, and we must add spiritual gifts to this list. Spiritual gifting is one of the windows through which to study and pursue spiritual growth. The controlling and core theme is Christian growth, and it can be viewed from these various perspectives. A doctrine of spiritual gifts should not be isolated from this core theme.

Each of the angles from which we can study and pursue maturing contributes important principles for our growth. The spiritual gifting angle contributes the individualized perspective: my spiritual development will look different than yours. That individualization is not disconnected from the other aspects of growth which we share in common. But, as we studied in chapter 7, carrying my cross will involve the development of my true self.

Integrating an understanding of spiritual gift development with our teaching about spiritual growth provides people with the motivating understanding that the fulfilling development of their unique identity and potential is part of that growth. In our teaching and mentoring, as well as in our personal journeys, let's connect the themes of growth and gifted potential.

It is commonly understood by people in general and in psychological research that personal potential develops along the journey of personal growth. Yet our popular doctrine of spiritual gifts has taught that certain potentials are added to us without respect to where we are in our development or maturing. This is contrary to wisdom and, as noted above, neglects that gifting is a metaphor.

It is not that, in our journeys, there is no supernatural intervention by God that affects our gifting. The most significant intervention is salvation, when we are baptized in the Spirit. The possibilities for the discovery, development, and use of our gifts can then be supercharged by walking in step with God's Spirit. Their use can then be developed to bring the most glory to God.

Blending our understanding of gifts and growth also yields a more holistic understanding of developing our potentials. My spiritual maturing needs to link to my progress in the psychological, intellectual, social, and practical or creative skills areas of my life. Development and use of my gifted potentials will require me to take concrete steps of growth in all these areas and more.

Along with intentional spiritual growth involvements, I may need to finish my college degree, or take an art course, or join a volunteer community effort, or get some counseling. The Journey View embraces development of the whole person in the process of developing full potential.

CHAPTER FOURTEEN

ROMANS & EPHESIANS

In earlier chapters of this book, life application of the Journey View has been the focus, particularly in parts 1 and 2. My purpose in this chapter and the next is to focus more on my interpretive conclusions in each of the four gifts passages in the New Testament Epistles. Yet, as stated in the introduction, you need the inputs from parts 1 through 3 to fill out the interpretations I share in part 4.

The interpretive factors explained in chapter 13 should also be studied as a context for understanding these thoughts on the specific gift passages. One of the topics considered there was the gift lists. The popular view, in its definition of gifts as added abilities, tends to be list focused.

In the Journey View, an individual's gift identification does not depend on defining those list entries, but rather on discernment of each person's uniqueness. Defining the entries is most useful for discerning the functional dynamics of a healthy church. Therefore, if you are looking for my definitions of those list entries, you will not find them in this chapter or this book. Many other publications do an excellent job of defining them.

With that clarification in mind, we will turn our attention to each of the four major gift passages in the New Testament. My purpose here is not to present detailed exegesis of each passage, though I am satisfied that the Journey View's interpretations do stand up to such careful study. What we will do here is to look at the interpretive highlights of each passage that together guide us to the different perspective on gifts presented in this book.

A PRIORITY SPOT FOR GIFTS

If you were teaching someone the basics of practical Christian living, would spiritual gifts be one of your first topics? In both Romans and Ephesians, it is for Paul. Unlike 1 Corinthians, those two letters are more formally arranged. Each letter starts with a major doctrinal section (Romans 1–11 and Ephesians 1–3) and follows it with an applied living section (Romans 12–16 and Ephesians 4–6). Spiritual gifts appear almost first in those applied sections.

It seems to me that the topic of gifts has an "also there" status in theology and biblical studies. This is consistent with the usual perspective of the popular view that gifts are utilitarian, and you get them as an additional benefit automatically at conversion.

Paul's prioritized placement of the topic in Romans and Ephesians implies there is something more central for us to grasp in understanding and living our spiritual giftedness. The Journey View's focus on metaphor and spiritual growth brings the topic of gifts to a more prominent place in understanding biblical living in community and individual maturing. It implies that gifts are not only about avenues of serving but how those tasks arise out of one's Christian identity development.

In both Ephesians 4:1–6 and Romans 12:1–2, Paul headlines certain umbrella themes for his applicational sections, and then indicates that a fundamental application of correct Christian theology will be living out spiritual gift potential in a body context (Ephesians 4:7–16; Romans 12:3–8). First, we follow this in Romans 12.

ROMANS 12

In Romans 12:1–2 we are charged to respond to God's mercy. The focus on mercy comes right out of the previous context (11:30–32), summarizes chapters 1–11, and draws us to unreserved worship and denial of the pressure to conform to what this world wants us to be. When we studied cross wisdom in chapters 3 and 7, we learned that pressures to conform and imitate are at odds with living as the unique gifted persons we each are. In this lead-in to spiritual gifts in Romans, here is that idea again.

This kind of response to mercy positions us for God's work to begin within us: transforming us by renewing our minds (12:2). In our journeys of transforming and resisting conforming, Paul indicates we are going to discover God's will.[1]

Some interpreters see Paul selecting, in most of the rest of Romans (12:3–15:13), what he wants to emphasize about how our transforming lives display God's will.[2] The apostle starts that emphasis with the command to have an accurate self-concept (12:3) and live as the diversely gifted and interdependent body of Christ (12:4–8).

The hinge between the ideas of accurate self-concept and diversely gifted body is the phrase "each according to the measure of faith that God has assigned" (12:3), which seems to be Paul's expression for the unique persons that lie behind the metaphor of gifts.[3] The interdependence of those people is a key feature of God's "good and acceptable and perfect" will (12:2), and their diversity expresses grace (12:6).

There are seven gifts listed in 12:6–8, but only three of them show up in any of the other gift lists in the Epistles. This flexibility underlines that the apostle isn't speaking from any standardized list of gifts; rather his perspective of how to describe and categorize the grace-diversity of God's people easily varies from occasion to occasion.

The Romans passage then (beginning in 12:9) echoes the movement we saw from 1 Corinthians 12 to 13, giving priority to *agape* for living interdependently as gifted persons. In chapter 4 we looked at the application of this "sincere" love in relationships that powerfully help us in our journeys of gift development.

It takes the kind of love described in 12:9–13 to embrace unique others, affirming their differing strengths without exalting certain people. Yet that love challenges the evil that corrupts unique expressions of grace (12:9 cf. 1 Corinthians 13:6). That is a strategic ministry I need from my brothers and sisters in Christ because of the battles I need to fight to further develop my giftedness.

Sincere love shows honor for and devotion to others (12:10) who, in this context, serve God differently than I serve God. My experience is that this is quite a stretch for myself and others to do! But when we receive such love, it encourages us to hope-filled endurance (12:12), which we need as we each pursue our unique missions. My focus here is to help us perceive the *agape* qualities listed in this passage as relevant to developing the diverse giftedness also taught in these verses.

But perhaps *the biggest takeaway from the Romans presentation about gifts is that transformation flows into gifted diversity. That is, my spiritual maturing and the discovery, development, and use of my gifts are linked.* This integration of spiritual growth with spiritual gifts is a key characteristic of the Journey View, and I have also pointed it out, and will again, as it occurs in 1 Corinthians and Ephesians. People develop their giftedness within the process of maturation.

EPHESIANS 4

I already noted that Romans and Ephesians are more formally arranged presentations of doctrine and practice than most of Paul's letters. In 1 Corinthians we must contextualize our interpretations of his teachings about gifts with the situational problems he is addressing in that church. In Romans and Ephesians, we do not have indication of specific church circumstances that color what Paul has to say about gifts.

In fact, Ephesians is generally understood as a circular letter, intended to be passed among the several churches of Asia Minor.[4] This suggests that what Paul has to say about gifts in this Epistle is broadly applicable to all churches and focuses on what is most essential to know about spiritual gifts.

This is not to say that the situationally influenced gift teachings of 1 Corinthians are any less authoritative scripture than Ephesians and Romans. But if we are constructing a theology of spiritual gifts for belief and practice, it nudges us to discern which elements of biblical teaching are foundational concerning gifts, and which are built on that foundation.

We shouldn't simplistically say this Epistle contributes foundational ideas and that one doesn't, but we do need to factor in that the occasion of each letter matters for our interpretation.[5] The relevance of cross wisdom in 1 Corinthians is broadly applicable for all of us in dealing with gifted diversity (see chapters 3 and 15).

Yet the more compact, formal, and broadly intended presentation on gifts in Ephesians needs to be heard as if Paul's attitude is this: "If you only learn certain truths about gifts, here's what you should learn."[6]

The Ephesians Gift List

Two features of this Ephesians presentation are intriguing, then, within this understanding. Let's think first about the gift list Paul offers here, which is contained within one verse (4:11). It is his shortest list, and he only lists people who are gifted in various kinds of leadership. It's not that he doesn't think we're all gifted. He echoes Romans 12:6 when he writes that "grace was given to each one of us according to the measure of Christ's gift" (4:7).

Apparently, *Paul doesn't think that providing these churches with names of the gifts received by the majority of people is important.* His focus here is that people with leadership gifts "equip the saints for the work of ministry, for building up the body of Christ" (4:12). He goes on to stress our unity, our maturing, and how, in the metaphor of the body, we each serve as the unique part we are (4:13–16).

If serving as who I uniquely am depends on knowing what the specified gifts are (beyond leaders), Paul has dropped the ball, and the churches of Asia Minor are at a real disadvantage. But no, contrary to the popular view's usual emphasis, the gift lists are not foundational for our understanding of spiritual gifting. The apostle deems it strategically sufficient to teach Christians that they are each individually contributing members of the body of Christ and that gifted leaders equip them for their ministries.

The other point to note in 4:11 is that Paul listed variously gifted leadership people, rather than listing them simply as gifts or abilities that are given. In his gift lists, he flexibly moves around in his descriptions: activities, abilities, potentials, qualities, ministries, roles or offices, areas of service, and supernatural manifestations.

This flexibility in the mode of expression, along with the fluctuations in what gifts are listed in each Epistle, suggests Paul was describing his observations of diverse people and their ways of serving, not revealing to us new abilities we get at salvation. His perspectives shifted somewhat from occasion to occasion because that is what commonly happens when someone is categorizing, particularly if standardization is not necessary.

These flexibilities fit better with understanding the lists as containing category headings (mentioned in chapter 13) because categories are intermediate ways to identify people, not fine-tuned and specific to unique individuals. We will discuss that further in chapter 16, but a key point here is that in writing this broadly intended letter, Paul considered the categorizing of all the non-leadership gifted people as optional or unnecessary.

Emphasis on Spiritual Growth

What does Paul consider non-optional or necessary when teaching about gifts? In the contexts (and/or canonical connections) of each of his spiritual gift passages, the themes of a) unity amid diversity, b) spiritual growth, and c) the truth-in-love dynamic in relationships are important.

I previously covered how contextual studies in each of Paul's gift passages emphasize these themes and have given these three values priority in the Journey View. But I have especially underlined that this view integrates spiritual gifting with spiritual growth.

That integration has not been commonly recognized, particularly in 1 Corinthians and Romans. But in 1 Corinthians, we saw that diverse gifting (1 Corinthians 12) needs the application of cross wisdom (1 Corinthians 1), and clearly this involves Paul challenging his readers to grow spiritually (1:10; 3:1). In Romans, gifting flows out of our ongoing transformation (12:1). And the apostle's emphasis on *agape* in tandem with gifts, in both those letters, implies the need for growth in love to realize our spiritual gift potential.

The second intriguing feature of the Ephesians gifts presentation is *how* Paul points to spiritual growth. Everybody agrees that spiritual maturing is prominent in Ephesians 4:1–16, though the popular view usually sees gifts as utilitarian for the outcome of spiritual growth (individual and corporate)[7] rather than integrating gifting and growth as in the Journey View. But because of one unique way that growth is connected with gifts in Ephesians, which I introduced in chapter 2, I want to revisit it here.

Heirs in Christ: Battles and Gifting

If we follow Paul's line of thinking when he starts talking about gifts in 4:7, we are quickly led by him to ponder the ascending Christ who, as a victorious warrior, has won gifts he now gives to us (4:8). The central assertion in this image is that Christ "led a host of captives," and that relates to "the measure of Christ's gift" (4:7) distributed to each of us. Paul intends that we would stop and ruminate on this story, much as we would linger to absorb the impact of an immersive historical or artistic display in a museum.

He has already capped off his opening exposition about God's eternal purpose to save us and make us heirs in Christ with the image of the ascended Christ seated far above all powers that challenged (1:20–23). When he closes his letter, he will exhort us to join Christ's army in the ongoing battles against those powers (6:10–17).[8] Here in the middle of the letter he is saying that our ministries in this age are empowered by the battle-won gifts within us.

Paul draws our attention to Jesus Christ. He is the giver of gifts because he led in the battles to retrieve those riches. He is the risen and enthroned King who has rightfully received these spoils, only to then distribute them as gifts to us.[9] And Paul did not make up this illustration or offer this military story without intending to enrich our understanding of gifting. He is a student of the Old Testament, and from there he knows that this is the story of God and his people.

The Old Testament Precedent[10]

He points us to a psalm that celebrates God as the Victorious Warrior ascending to his throne after centuries of leading his people in battles (Psalm 68). As we study this poem, we notice that the King's way is to receive spoils from his vanquished foes and then enrich his people with them (68:11–14, 18, 29).[11]

Throughout Israel's Old Testament journey, that scene is played out over and over again. There are over fifty stories, comments, commands, prayers, or prophecies that reference Israel either receiving spoils or being despoiled (see appendix 2). The story began when they left Egypt with plunder, continued in battles along the way to the promised land, and took on even more meaning as they conquered their inheritance one piece at a time.

Psalm 68 poetically celebrates this journey, and Paul wants us to think about this metanarrative when we think about Christ gifting us. The impact for us is intended to be inspiring and exciting. We are invited into the epic saga of Jesus Christ leading through battles into spoils-laden victories. And this can be your story because God has promised you an inheritance (Ephesians 1:11–18), just as he did Israel.

I noted in chapter 12 that the amount of explicit scriptural teaching about gifts is relatively limited, leaving us with a vacuum of understanding. The popular view fills this vacuum with its mechanical and utilitarian interpretation. Why not instead allow the emphasis on spiritual growth in the gift contexts, and this amazing spoils metaphor Paul imports, impact our understanding of spiritual gifts?

When we looked at the spoils journey in chapter 2, I quoted the Bible scholar who says that "For Paul, the OT is not primarily something to understand; rather, the OT itself creates understanding."[12] Paul intends his Psalms citation in Ephesians 4:8 to be an "aha!" moment for us, in which our understanding of gifting is filled in with the big story. It unfolded in Israel's history, and now it unfolds in our journeys as we follow the ascended and victorious Christ.

Further Points

Scholars debate the verb change in 4:8, where Paul wrote that God "gave" gifts instead of, as Psalm 68:18 indicates, God "received" gifts.[13] For our purposes here I will stress that in the psalm, the King distributes the spoils to his people after having received them from captives (68:11–13).[14] This enrichment of people through the ascending God, now Christ, is the main focus and common thread.[15]

In Ephesians 4:9–10 Paul elaborates on the ascent of Christ. These verses may be interpreted as a) reinforcing that Christ is referred to in 4:8, b) linking the Spirit who descended at Pentecost with the ascending Christ, or c) speaking of Christ's descent to and ascent from this earth.[16] The decision is not strategic for our studies of gifts, but I tend toward the third idea because it parallels Christ's battles on our behalf (during his earthly life) with God's presence with Israel in their battles.[17]

In chapter 1 I connected Peter's use of *poikilos* to describe grace as seen through gifts (1 Peter 4:10), with Paul's use of *polupoikilos* to describe God's wisdom as seen through the church (Ephesians 3:10). Paul's enthusiasm about the now revealed mystery that Gentiles and Jews are fellow-heirs in one body (3:3–6, 9; cf. 2:11–22) leads into his declaration that it was always God's intention that his super-variegated wisdom would be displayed through his people.

This context flows into his teaching on gifts in Ephesians 4:

- God's intention is that his variegated wisdom is seen through the church (3:10).
- This was his eternal purpose in Christ (3:11).
- May the Father strengthen you out of his glorious riches (3:16).
- Therefore, live in unity and love (4:1–6).
- And receive from Christ his variegated and rich spoils (4:7).

To conclude this chapter: in the Journey View, spiritual gifts are one of Paul's first life applications in Romans and Ephesians, based on his theological foundations, because he sees spiritual gifting as an important dimension of spiritual growth. See appendix 2 for further thoughts on the relevance of the spoils theme for spiritual gifting.

CHAPTER FIFTEEN

1 CORINTHIANS & 1 PETER

Unlike Romans and Ephesians, 1 Corinthians and 1 Peter are not arranged as formal treatises in which doctrinal foundation is followed by practical applications. Spiritual gifts come up in 1 Corinthians as part of a string of issues Paul needs to address in that church. Peter speaks to a variety of topics—including gifts—as he follows the theme of remaining faithful to Christ as born-again heirs in an unfriendly world. In these contexts, each contributes important insights for our understanding of spiritual gifts.

1 CORINTHIANS 12–13

The messages of this Epistle, as previously mentioned, are influenced by the problems in the church at Corinth and Paul's responses to those problems, prompted by the church's questions sent to him.

In my survey of this gift passage, I do not include 1 Corinthians 14. In Paul's responding mode, that chapter zooms in on thorny situations dealing with prophecy and tongues. In other words, he departs from laying out general principles about gifts in the church to take up a subtopic relevant to that church.

1 Corinthians 14 is an important chapter for churches dealing with those issues, but it goes beyond the scope of discerning the Bible's general view on the topic of gifts, which is what this book seeks to do. Also, the gifts Paul discusses in that chapter relate to the category of supernatural gifts, which I will address in chapter 17.

Two Major Metaphors

The Corinthian church is characterized both by serious schisms (1:10–13; 3:3–9; 11:18–19) and by supernatural spiritual manifestations (1:7; 12:8–10; 13:2, 8; 14:12, 26–31). These circumstances interact with each other, revealing that many are impressed with some people more than others in the church, and promoting that attitude.

Like a pastor, Paul appeals to these believers in many ways in 1 Corinthians, and perhaps climaxes his appeals in chapter 12 with asking them to imagine church as a body where every part is strategic—specifically, Christ's body. The apostle's strong focus in that chapter is about achieving unity amid the reality of diversity. The body metaphor responds to this acute need in Corinth, and in the metaphor, each individual is described as a body member (12:27).

The Corinthians were apparently calling the spiritual phenomena in their church *pneumatika* (12:1), but Paul wants them to focus on grace, so he immediately (beginning in 12:4) suggests what he feels is a better description of how the diverse body parts express themselves: *charismata*.[1]

The Corinthians needed, and we need, a godly rather than a worldly way (see 1:10–12, 18–21, 3:3–9) to look at our diverse styles of being and serving. To offer that to us, Paul adds to his descriptive metaphor of the body another layer of descriptive metaphor: the grace-gifted individual members of the body.[2]

Rather than reading into this text that Paul is introducing a doctrine about receiving new abilities, it seems best to approach Paul's words about gifts in 1 Corinthians 12 by perceiving that he is offering a second metaphor to alter how we look at our diversity (see chapter 13). Let's then note some characteristics of how Paul breaks out his perspective that we are diversely gifted in 12:4–11, 28–30.

Categories of Individuals

In 12:4–6, the main point is that all the diverse expressions have the same source ("same Spirit . . . same Lord . . . same God"). While Paul emphasizes unity of source, he creates a grid of categories—gifts, service, and activities—and lays it over the array of diverse spiritual expressions. He is beginning his efforts to mold and change his readers' perspectives about their diversity, and he comes up with categories (of a unified field) to do so.[3]

In 12:7–11, he signals that, though he is using categories, he is thinking about individuals, headlining that with this statement: "To each is given the manifestation of the Spirit for the common good" (12:7). The perspective described in the rest of the paragraph is that each individual is a manifester of the Spirit because each person is a recipient from the Spirit. You might picture the Spirit as a light inside a ball, and each person is a unique cut-out shape on the ball's surface.

We should not reify the language of being "given" (or the Spirit's "distribution" or "apportioning," 12:11) into a point-in-time transaction and then switch our focus away from persons to new abilities that are the things given. (See discussion of reification under Use of Metaphor in chapter 13.)

The phrases "To one ... to another ... to another ..." repeated in 12:8–10 keep our focus on gifted persons, not gifts per se. But of course Paul could not list every individual in his letter, so he is again using categorization to describe diversely gifted people.

When the popular view deals with 1 Corinthians 12, the focus is often on the gift lists themselves. It's interesting, though, that only six of this chapter's thirty-one verses list specific gifts (depending on how you interpret 12:4–6). Clarification of gift entities is not the focus. But within this brevity, when we move on from Paul's list in 12:8–10 to his list in 12:28–30, he shows us just how flexible he is in categorizing the diversity of grace-gifted people.

Flexible Categories

Both lists contain nine gifts, but only overlap in five.[4] The first emphasizes activities, though some are potentialities or perhaps qualities (e.g., faith). The second list uses "personal categories"[5] in some entries. In other words, he lists gifted persons or perhaps offices; and he includes some abilities or areas of service. And some of the entries in both lists clearly involve supernatural manifestations.

Let's note some observations about these lists:

- Paul doesn't think it's important to define each list entry, though a lot of attention is put on definitions in popular presentations.
- It is difficult to characterize the various types of entries.
- The modes of expression can change from list to list (e.g., prophecy to prophets).
- The same list of entries does not occur to the same author, even within the same letter.

This picture of flexibility in listing gifts carries over into Romans, Ephesians, and 1 Peter. In my view, this reinforces that the apostles a) did not receive by revelation any official list of gifts, and b) were observing and describing groups of people using the metaphor of gifting and the tool of categorization. Therefore, uniformity of gift lists was not a priority. Varying categorical schemes came to the apostles' minds each time they decided to teach about diverse gifting.

Commenting on the gift lists in 1 Corinthians 12, D. A. Carson mentions characteristics of those lists, such as:

- None of the lists, including those in other Epistles, "should be taken as exhaustive."
- "The order of the gifts varies considerably."
- "Paul would not have been uncomfortable with spiritual gifts made up of some mix of so-called natural talent—what he would consider still to be God's gift—and of specific, Spirit-energized endowment."
- "The close relationships among the gifts of faith, healings, and miracles again suggests that the entries on the list [Carson seems to mean all of them] are not quantum packages, each discrete from the others."[6]

It is my belief that the best understanding of the list entries we can draw from these exegetical insights is that they are categories, and the "data" being categorized are people. The headings Paul uses for the categories make them center-bounded sets. This means they together form a spectrum (continuum), in which the categories blend from one to the next and to the next.

Gifts and the Cross

In chapter 3 I presented applications of cross wisdom for living with our corporate gifted diversity. I believe we are to read the wisdom about the body and gifts, in 1 Corinthians 12, in light of the cross wisdom that is explained in 1 Corinthians 1.

Paul's focus on the cross there is rooted, of course, in the actual cross of Christ. Jesus' attitudes in carrying his cross, and his call to us to carry our crosses, are part of the wisdom of the cross that is to give us understanding about living in our unique giftedness.

Thus, our thinking about spiritual gifts is contextualized by canonical connections, both within 1 Corinthians and then to the Gospels (e.g., Mark 8:34) and Hebrews (12:1–2). This contextualization points us to a Christocentric understanding of spiritual gifts. The particulars of these biblical connections are presented in chapters 3 and 7.

The Priority of Love

The other foundational contribution about gifts in the Corinthian letter is Paul's stress on *agape* in his chapter 13. While all four New Testament gift passages mention love in their contexts, the theme rises to particular importance in 1 Corinthians, as it is placed in contrast to their fascination with impressive gifts (13:1–3).

What I have suggested to you, particularly in chapter 4, is that the scripturally prescribed environment for gift discovery and development is sincere and powerful love. To a church needing guidance for living with their own—and one another's—giftedness, Paul prescribes *agape*. And his prescription is broken out into details in 1 Corinthians 13.

It is not wrong to offer spiritual gift classes and tests. But that is not what Scripture emphasizes as the best environment to learn about gifts. We are pointed to *agape* environments. We emphasized that in chapter 4, saw it applied specifically through listening in chapter 8, and thought about it as fleshed out through small groups in chapter 10 (see also worksheet 1). Paul thought it deserved a lot of focus in 1 Corinthians, and we should follow his lead.

1 PETER 4

In Peter's first Epistle, he encourages believers to persevere in their Christian living and testimony in the midst of persecution. Within that purpose, he introduces his own metaphors of the community of believers, drawing heavily on Old Testament images: living stones, spiritual house, holy and royal priesthood, holy nation (2:4–10).

He underlines the alien identity Christians have in this world, so that we will live distinctly from the world (2:11–12). Thus, Peter's parallel to the body concept of Paul is a community metaphor which deals with the tension of relationship with God while still in this world, rather than on the internal workings of the community (2:9–12).

But toward the end of this letter, Peter emphasizes that we must live in light of Christ's return (4:7, 13, 17–18; 5:1, 4, 6, 10). In the context of that theme added to the theme of suffering as Christians, Peter speaks to how believers relate to one another. His brief words about using our gifts to serve others flow out of his command to "love each other deeply" (4:8 NIV) in these end times (4:7).

Variegated Grace

Previously, we focused on Peter's adjective *poikilos*, learning in chapter 1 that it was especially used of artwork and usually denotes variegated colors.[7] From this I have spoken of God's spectrum of grace. In thinking of how the diversity of God's people displays his grace and wisdom, both Peter and Paul reached for the colorful *poikilos* (1 Peter 4:10; Ephesians 3:10).

The people-centered, rather than gift-centered, Journey View is not based on a lexical analysis of *poikilos*. It is based on the interpretations of gifts and gifting as metaphor and the gift lists as categories of people. But *poikilos*, suggesting "spectrum of grace," is illustrative and corroborative of these interpretations. It suggests a variety of (persons as) grace-expressions that no list can contain except through categorization.

Before we analyze this diversity into a list of categories, however, poikilos *asks us to synthesize it in an image.* We are invited to imaginatively enjoy the wonder of God's creativity. It is a picture of beauty, intended to take our breath away. I earlier suggested the image of a prism, through which the grace and wisdom of God is refracted into the many hues we are that each reflect God uniquely.[8] How many? I'd say *poikilos* suggests that it's myriad, not limited like any list of spiritual gifts (categories) must be.

Peter also used *poikilos* when he referred to the variety of trials we face in our lives (1 Peter 1:6), as did James (James 1:2). They both depict those diverse trials as positives because they contribute to the maturing of our faith. We've focused on how battles must be fought in the development of who we each uniquely are (chapters 2 and 6). In God's wisdom, he uses a spectrum of trials in our lives as he develops us into the spectrum of his grace that we collectively are.[9]

Peter's Take on Gifts

Perhaps the most prominent feature of the popular view of gifts is that it collects all the mentioned gifts in the New Testament and attempts to consolidate them into one list. This method is based on the idea that the gifts are entities added to each of us. In this view, our need is to come up with a list of those added abilities that is as complete as possible[10] so we can use it to discern which new abilities we've received.

If we didn't have Peter's input, we'd already have our hands full coming up with that composite list, just based on the fluidity in Paul's four lists. But the popular view tackles that, and then adds on Peter's list of two gifts (speaking and serving, 4:11). What's wrong with this picture? Surely Peter knew of other gifts and ministries. This apostle's very brief list is an indication that the popular view's conception of what gifts are is missing something.

In the Journey View, the list entries are category headings, and the categories are filled with gifted people—not gifts per se or added abilities. Peter's short list can best be explained this way. He is categorizing people.

We will discuss categorization and its implications in the next chapter. But Peter and Paul categorize differently, don't they? That's interesting. My wife and I categorize differently. I'll bet you and your best friend categorize differently. Different brains applied to the same task will do the task differently. We see that variation between Paul and Peter. We even see that Paul will vary his perspective on gift categories from one time to another.

Many authors have done insightful character studies of people in the Bible, and Peter and Paul are depicted as having different personalities. One of the characteristics noted about Paul, from his writings, is that he can be quite analytical as he breaks out all the details of a doctrine he is teaching (see Romans 6). From the Gospels, we learn about Peter as the disciple who is quick to speak, in bursts of idealism (see Matthew 17:4; 26:33).

The point is that Peter is brief and non-analytical. He creates two broad categories of gifted people—speaking people and serving people—thinking that this generalization is valid and sufficient. He probably felt that *poikilos* in the previous verse strongly enough made the point that God's grace has a myriad of expressions through gifted people. Meanwhile, Paul felt it would be helpful to break down the varieties of *charismata* into smaller and more specified categories. Both are right. Both are useful.

The Metaphor Applied

Yet though they have different angles and ways of presenting this topic, both apostles write within the metaphor of gifting (see chapter 13). The two premier apostles of the early church are both teaching this metaphor as a way to perceive God's diversified grace through his people.

They further agree that this metaphor is to inspire us to concrete acts of serving one another. Paul uses the body metaphor and his focus on *agape* to stress that. Peter also sees use of our gifts as linked to practical expressions of love (1 Peter 4:8–9), and then our responsibility is to be good stewards of the gift-grace we've each received, sourced in God's power as we serve one another (4:10–11).

The flow of grace from God is refracted into a myriad of hues on his spectrum of grace, and he is glorified by this beauty. Then each of we hues faithfully allow that grace to keep flowing through us, serving others with words and strength that come from God "in order that in everything God may be glorified through Jesus Christ. To him belong glory and dominion forever and ever. Amen" (1 Peter 4:11).

CHAPTER SIXTEEN

CATEGORIES VS UNIQUENESS

It seems that, by default, our brains categorize information, things, and people. Some personalities do it more than others, some do it more consciously than others, and we have differing styles of doing it. But we all do it because it helps us make sense of what or who we encounter and navigate through the responsibilities of life.

When it comes to people categories, we often find they are enlightening and fun to use! You may have used some of the many popular tools that help you understand the personality or strengths of yourself and others. Those tools perhaps gave you insights to make you more successful in relationships and projects and made for enjoyable discussions with friends.

Categorization is also commonly used to help people discern their spiritual gifts. Many popular publications about gifts encourage it when they define the various gift list entries and provide tests to help you determine which gifts you have. They may or may not call it categorization, but it functions like that.

In earlier chapters I've written that the Journey View sees the gift list entries as category headings rather than added abilities, and the categories are populated with people. In this view, categorizing people is not bad to do—the biblical authors did it—and there are values to be gained from it today. But in this view of gifting, we place the emphasis elsewhere because we don't think the emphasis of the scriptural message about gifts is on the lists (categories) themselves.

The Journey View instead highlights that each person is unique and is invited to their journey of growth into fuller expression of their giftedness. In this chapter, we'll learn that if we use people categories, we shouldn't think we're done once we've categorized ourselves and others, even if we've also guided people into roles that fit their gifts, personalities, passions, or other identifiers.

That's because the Journey View integrates gifting with growth and teaches that one way to describe the aim of your growth is to become more and more the unique expression of God's grace that you are. We move through and beyond categorization. We engage with one another's growth in our gifting journeys. We learn, pay attention to, and affirm the unique ways each of us can manifest God in this world.

Most of us instinctively feel that each person is unique, even if we see that, more or less, we fit into certain categories.[1] But as individuals and as churches, do we respond and relate to one another as if we're each unique expressions of God? Or do we stop at categorization? Since this tension between uniqueness and categorization is relevant to the topic of spiritual gifts, let's look further into what we need to know about it.

CATEGORIZATION CAVEATS

Whether you categorize people using a formal instrument made for that purpose, or just informally in your own mind, be aware of the following factors involved in any categorizing. If you forget these qualifiers when you're categorizing people, you may draw wrong conclusions about them.

First, a category is an abstract concept. To see and gain the benefit of a people category, you must stop considering one individual and move to considering a range of individuals. Your attention shifts from this unique person in front of you to the characteristics that a certain range of people seem to share in common. That is a shift from the concrete to the abstract, and it comes with benefits and cautions, which we'll explore further below.

Second, those abstract concepts we call categories are someone's theory and perspective. There are multiple theories about how, and perspectives from which, to categorize people. We can learn a lot from these many different angles on understanding people types. But we need to remember that these perspectives are not set in stone.

However, I do need to qualify that point. I've said the scriptural writers used categories when they listed spiritual gifts. It is my belief that Scripture is divinely inspired and authoritative right down to its words and sentences. In that way, then, those lists are set in stone, setting them off from other human categorization schemes.

Obviously, however, they're not set in stone if that means they should be rigidly and exactly replicated every time they show up in the Bible. We've already considered Paul's fluctuating lists and the difference between his and Peter's lists. Varying perspectives were at work, and we've drawn conclusions from that in earlier pages. Later I will say more about these scriptural categories.

Third, a theory of people categories is a template or grid placed over a continuum of people. In using people categories, we sometimes lose sight of the fact that what we're really dealing with is a lot of unique individuals, all scattered along a continuum. Our grid of categories is a theoretical tool to help us think about all that diversity. The reality is unique individuals, and no categorization of an individual can give you full understanding of him or her.

I previously stated that the popular view has reified the metaphor of gifts and gifting, mistakenly interpreting those as concrete. We should be aware that reification is also a risk whenever people categories are used. When we lose sight of unique individuals and think mainly of the categories we're using to understand people or describe diversity, we are slipping toward the error of reification.

CATEGORIZATION CAUTIONS

Remember the ministry team meeting we visited in chapter 7? We had ten or eleven people on our team, but we specifically met Antonia, Kyrsten, and Beckett, along with Jaden and his wife, Kimberley. Let's say I want our team to get to know one another better and function more smoothly in teamwork. I could use both a spiritual gifts inventory and a personality test to help with that.

This decision is a good idea because if we pay more attention to the varying strengths of those on the team, we can appreciate each person's contribution and experience more harmony and effectiveness together. As the leader, I could administer the tests, share the results, and give the team some training to understand and use the insights. Given the characters on our team, we'd probably have a lot of fun too!

In that kind of setting, it's important for us to realize that what we are doing is categorizing unique individuals (not discerning added-on gifts) and to remember the three caveats about categorizing we just surveyed.

Also, instead of using these tools as a stand-alone way to learn about each individual and promote teamwork, we would see their use as part of a bigger process of each team member's growth into their unique gifted self. Based on all these considerations, we can move forward in this categorizing, honoring the following cautions.

First, don't leave someone with less than what they need. Let's say I've categorized Antonia: the test results say she has the gifts of encouragement and wisdom, and her personality is highlighted with characteristics of being a discerning challenger and a friend for the long haul. Those are insights for Antonia and her teammates. It is knowledge—mainly about how Antonia thinks and how she acts. But is there more to know about Antonia? And how much has this helped Antonia feel known?

Those are important questions because God didn't create a discerning challenger with gifts of encouragement and wisdom; he created Antonia. Her need is to develop her gifted uniqueness. Categorization is helpful, but it falls short of discerning her uniqueness. As her team leader, I can point Antonia toward using various resources, especially an inner circle, to support the development of her true self.[2]

Second, don't miss the truth about each person. Beckett, to no one's surprise, turned out to be an adventurous extrovert with gifts of serving and exhortation. Through categorizing, we've narrowed down what Beckett is. Notice I didn't say "who" Beckett is. We didn't go that far. And stopping there is like determining there is hidden treasure in a certain acre of land and feeling satisfied with that.

Will I take seriously that each person is a unique statement of God's grace? Will I miss the unique hue on God's spectrum of grace and wisdom that Beckett is? C. S. Lewis wrote that it is my job to discern and bear the weight of glory that is bestowed on my neighbor.[3] We, as Beckett's teammates, have the responsibility to discern and be fascinated with his glory.

Third, don't ignore uniqueness to fit a role. We've become most familiar with Jaden, and you'll remember that my expectations of his fit into our ministry came into conflict with his developing uniqueness. Jaden's test results showed he is a spontaneous artist-type with gifts of speaking and leading.

In my early connections with Jaden, I focused on his journey into his potentials. But as he grew and served, I started thinking about myself and the wants I have (in this case, the success of the ministry I lead). That distorted my perception of Jaden. I saw what I wanted to see. This is usually more of a problem with the informal categorizing we do in our heads than it is with using formal instruments to categorize. But we can put ourselves and our needs ahead of the other using either kind of categorizing.

Finally, don't settle for short-term investment. Using categorizing tools can be an event. Sometimes churches offer short-term classes to learn about gifts and take tests. But gifting is a journey, and in this book, we've studied many aspects of that journey, including battles and persevering friends. That's what it takes to grow and unearth those buried potentials.

Kimberley's tests revealed that she is a detail-oriented organizer with gifts of giving and mercy. She tends to be a quiet person, but she sought out my wife because she sensed her need to grow further into being the unique woman God created her to be. Over the next few years, Susan walked alongside Kimberley and Kyrsten, helping them discern and tackle the battles they needed to fight to recover the rich spoils God intended for them.

INTERMEDIATE TOOLS

The point to remember when you use categorization to understand people, or give understanding to them, is that it is intermediate. Whether you are using personality tests, strength assessments, spiritual gift inventories, or just categorizing others in your head, you are not fully knowing those you are categorizing.

Developing a fuller understanding requires loving listening and a longer-term relationship. In addition, categorization can only go so far in helping others go deeper in discerning who they are. Discovery, development, and display of our potentials is a multidimensional journey. This book is about that Journey View of gifting.

Yet categorization can be a helpful intermediate tool. I've grown to understand myself more thoroughly by using personality tests and gift inventories. In today's world, there are many different people-categorizing tools available, each coming from its own particular angle. They offer diverse and nuanced insights about our personal characteristics.

It is beyond the scope of this book to survey the many tools available and comment on their features and values. An Internet search on spiritual gifts, personality types, strengths assessment, and similar topics will yield an abundance of information and options. But beyond the categorization caveats and cautions already mentioned, when you consider specific tools for your use, let me offer some perspectives to keep in mind.

First, in the Journey View interpretation of spiritual gifts, our focus is on the potentials you were born with as a unique person created by God. The many tools available to assess your personal characteristics, in that view, are all trying to discern those potentials. They are all likely to have some level of value in doing that. Further, instruments that clarify people's positive strengths help us appreciate diverse types of people instead of judging some types as better than others.

Second, every tool is based on decisions made by its developers about what is most important. Some instruments will focus on variations in basic cognitive functioning (e.g., extroversion and introversion); others prioritize categories that apply in certain environments (e.g., work or groups). And then there are others that deal with relational effectiveness (e.g., styles of giving and receiving love).

Third, since every tool has its angle among many angles, there isn't one that captures the whole person. The wonder of each beautiful hue on God's spectrum of grace ultimately eludes categorization. That's why we each get a unique new name one day (Revelation 2:17).

Fourth, having said that, instruments with greater levels of complexity move in a direction toward uniqueness. But they also require more training for their administration and interpretation.

Finally, some categorizing tools are based on philosophies that may be at odds with Christian teaching in some areas. Whether this compromises the usefulness of an instrument is usually a debated topic among Christians. For example, the Enneagram has become very popular. Yet some Christians find that its origins and assumptions make it unsuitable for their use. For years, I have benefited from insights gained from another assessment tool based on Carl Jung's research, even though I don't agree with some important aspects of his philosophy.

Such instruments will often yield valuable insights and can be used without buying into the non-Christian views with which they're associated. But that is a decision you'll have to research and make when you're selecting tools for your use.

AGAPE DISCOVERS UNIQUENESS

Without love, there is no true knowing of the other person, the other person never feels known, and we miss the unique person they are on God's spectrum of grace. That's because it's only when we love, with the listening love we studied earlier, that we pay attention at the level needed to achieve those ends.

Categorization is easier than *agape*. It has its place. But when our knowing of people stops at categorization, we never discover the amazing treasure each person is. That's true whether we're using secular categories or Christian categories.

After writing about spiritual gifts, Paul continues: "And I will show you a still more excellent way" (1 Corinthians 12:31). Then he dives into *agape*. There is a search involved in discovering uniqueness, and love—moving beyond categorization—commits itself to that search. Read 1 Corinthians 13:4–7 again with that in mind.

Now since we are each in process, hopefully on the journey of retrieving our spoils and fighting the necessary battles along the way, the uniqueness of each of us is not yet as obvious as it will later become.

> Beloved, we are God's children now, and what we will be has not yet appeared; but we know that when he appears we shall be like him, because we shall see him as he is. (1 John 3:2)

It is at that moment of seeing Jesus that, in becoming fully like him, we arrive fully at who we each are.[4] He sees and names you uniquely, for his *agape* has sought you and discovered your uniqueness.

> To the one who conquers I will give . . . a white stone, with a new name written on the stone that no one knows except the one who receives it. (Revelation 2:17)

This conquering can partially be understood as the result of obeying his call to follow him by denying your false self and identifying and carrying your unique cross/mission (Mark 8:34). Perseverance in this process is not easy. Walking this journey is challenging. In chapter 7 we studied the example of Jesus, who denied the pressure to choose a false self, lived his unique identity, and pursued his unique mission.

It is ultimately love that empowers such a journey. Love is not content with categorization. Your love will pursue the unique and authentic me, will communicate your belief in me, and will help empower me for my unique mission. We must give such love to one another mutually, and each give it to ourselves as well. And our love for God pulls us forward toward becoming the unique persons he desires us each to be.

In sharing love these ways, we are echoing God's transcendent and eternal love for each of us. His love has prepared that white stone reception for each one who follows Jesus. We learned in chapter 6 how this vision of becoming our fully restored selves can pull us forward through the battles in our journeys.

SCRIPTURE'S CATEGORY LISTS

We are to approach the gifts lists in the Epistles with all these considerations in mind. They are scripture, but that is not inconsistent with seeing them as intermediate categories of people, which is consistent with interpreting gifts and gifting as metaphor. Honoring these lists as scriptural also is not inconsistent with acknowledging apostolic flexibility in presenting differing but overlapping category lists from place to place.

These scriptural lists also display another common characteristic of categorization noted above: every tool is based on decisions made by its developers about what is most important. When Paul and Peter devised their lists, they were prioritizing local churches. Therefore, their people categories reflect their purpose of application to local churches. This is a limiting and defining purpose, and an important purpose.

We might say that the lists are about Christians "doing" church and creating healthy church. That does not mean that the ways of serving listed do not also frequently overlap into other relationships. But the apostles were thinking about churches when they devised the lists.

That distinctive flavor of these lists sits alongside their contexts and canonical connections, which we have interpreted as teaching that gifting is about individuals on their journeys of growth. The lists show us what healthy church looks like when many gifted Christians are together discovering, developing, and using their unique potentials to serve one another.

I will leave it to other books to delve into these important pictures of healthy church. These lists are authoritative, apostolic wisdom for churches. But the main scene of individual gifting is journey.

CHAPTER SEVENTEEN

MANIFESTATIONS OF THE SPIRIT

When we see the diversity of gifts and activities of serving, we are seeing the Holy Spirit manifested through every one of us (1 Corinthians 12:4–7). The Spirit is the Person empowering all these expressions of God's grace (12:8–11). The Journey View affirms this while also affirming that a scriptural understanding of spiritual gifts is Christocentric rather than Spirit-centered.

THE SPIRIT AND/OR JESUS?[1]

The presence of the Holy Spirit was huge for the early church because of how acutely they felt the absence of Jesus. Anticipating this, Jesus clearly and reassuringly promised his followers that his Spirit would come following his departure.[2] In their transition from having Jesus physically present to what came next, we see in the book of Acts that they cherished the reality of the Holy Spirit affirming that Jesus was still with them in reality.

For all of the emphasis on the Spirit in Acts, however, Jesus seems to get more emphasis. The story of the Messiah, his rejection and resurrection, and his gospel message is what the apostles and followers of Christ all point to, even as they are empowered by his Spirit to do so.[3] All of the New Testament letters point to Christ, more than they point to the Spirit. And yet most of them find it important to teach us truth about the Holy Spirit.

Theologians have usually stressed, when teaching the doctrine of the Holy Spirit, that his role is to point to Jesus, not to himself. The Spirit is strategic and essential for us because we need the presence of Jesus.

When we come to New Testament teachings about spiritual gifts, this basic understanding is reflected. There is an acknowledgement that all giftedness manifests, or gives evidence of, the Spirit. Yet when he is mentioned in the texts about gifts, the emphasis seems to not stop there, but to be in movement toward Christ.

In Ephesians 4 Paul zooms in on Christ the Victorious Warrior as the giver of gifts, while also mentioning the Spirit in the context (4:1–10). Then his focus moves on to how we're Christ's diversely membered body. In Romans 12, the Spirit is not mentioned; the giver of gifts is God, and again his focus is on being Christ's body (12:1–13). Elsewhere in Romans, though, Paul has a lot to teach us about the Holy Spirit.[4] Peter does not mention the Spirit in connection with spiritual gifts.

A lot of publications about gifts point us to focus on the Holy Spirit. Generally, that is because of what we read in 1 Corinthians and Acts.

SUPERNATURAL GIFTS[5]

Especially prominent in Acts is how the giving of God's Spirit is often attested by the recipients miraculously speaking in tongues.

After this happened preeminently at Pentecost, it strategically recurred various times as evidence that the gospel and its blessings were extending beyond just those with Jewish heritage.[6] In that and other ways, the Spirit of Jesus empowered the spread of his gospel, including through supernatural events such as healings.[7]

Christians today hold varying beliefs about whether to use those wonderful miracles in Acts as a precedent for what we should experience today. Of course, those disagreements sometimes become the main scene when it comes to discussions about spiritual gifts. It is not only the Journey View that sees that issue as a distraction from what the scriptures emphasize about gifts. Kenneth Berding's alternative view (see chapter 12) implies the same by shifting the emphasis to ministry roles.

It is a valid question, however, to anyone who presents a view of spiritual gifts, to ask how those that seem to involve supernatural activity fit into their view. The question is valid regardless of whether you believe those gifts are still active today or not. Since I have presented that gifting is metaphorical, the gift lists are categories of people, and gifting is contingent on growth, I must answer the question in the context of this Journey View.

I've mentioned the occurrence of supernatural gifts in the narratives of Acts, but we encounter direct teaching about those gifts in 1 Corinthians. Due to that, I will mostly answer this question through use of Paul's teachings there. He does not mention those gifts in either Romans or Ephesians.

RESPONSE TO CORINTH

In earlier chapters we noted, and many biblical interpreters have taught, that in 1 Corinthians Paul is largely responding to the circumstances in and questions from the church at Corinth. We understand, therefore, that in addressing the topic of spiritual gifts beginning in chapter 12, Paul is responding to questions, confusions, and disagreements that exist in Corinth about gifts.

In 1 Corinthians 14 he deals in detail with struggles they're having with gifts of prophecy and tongues. But in chapters 12 and 13, as Paul teaches more broadly on the theme of gifts, he is wanting to shift the Corinthians' focus from their fascination with spiritual manifestations to the themes of grace-gifts for all, unity and diversity in the body of Christ, and love as the more excellent way.

One of the ways he leads in that shift is that, after starting with the Corinthians' preferred term *pneumatika* to speak of gifts, he promotes the term *charismata*. He is not teaching that *pneumatika* is a wrong idea; he returns to that term with guidance and affirmations in chapter 14. But he wants their focus to be on the grace-expressions of everyone rather than the attention-getting spiritual expressions of a few.

Parallel to that, Paul mentions the Spirit a lot in 12:1–13, but not at all in the rest of the chapter. His focus shifts to the body of Christ. We saw earlier (chapter 3) how this wisdom of Christ's body is to be read in light of the wisdom of Christ's cross from his chapter 1. I believe Paul wants the Corinthians, and us, to focus more on Christ than on the Spirit when we think about spiritual gifts.

Yet Paul starts with and uses their focus on *pneumatika* and the Spirit to begin his guidance to them. One way he does that is to gather all the diverse ways people are serving into one broad category called manifestations of the Spirit: "To each is given the manifestation of the Spirit for the common good" (12:7).

You are right, he is saying, to see the Spirit manifesting himself through spiritual gifts. But in this teaching, he is elevating all spiritual gifts—not just the attention-getting ones—to that status. He goes on to underline that repeatedly in his first gift list in 12:8–11.[8]

A BROAD NET OF PEOPLE CATEGORIES

I am suggesting that at the beginning of his discussion of gifts, Paul casts a very broad net to cover all of the ways the Spirit is manifested through God's people, correcting the Corinthians' narrower focus. He first calls that broad net manifestations of the Spirit, even though he is moving toward *charismata* as the preferred broad designation.

Apparently, the Corinthians already know that miracles and prophecy and tongues and healings and such are manifestations of the Spirit. Paul wants them to know that faith, utterances of wisdom, apostles, teachers, helping, administration and other gifts are also manifestations of the Spirit. Do you notice (in 12:8–10 and 12:28–30) he mixes together activities, abilities, roles, offices, people, and supernatural powers in this broad net? They're all manifestations of the Spirit.

And they're all *charismata*—spiritual gifts—which I have taught in this book is a metaphor that refers to the diversity of potential-filled individuals God has created. In that way, whether we are talking about individuals gifted with helps or gifted with tongues, we are talking about categories of people. Whether we're talking about those gifted with healings or with administration, we're talking about categories of people.

Paul demarcates and enumerates diverse categories of people in the church:

> To one is given through the Spirit the utterance of wisdom, and to another the utterance of knowledge according to the same Spirit, to another faith by the same Spirit, to another gifts of healing by the one Spirit, to another the working of miracles, to another prophecy, to another the ability to distinguish between spirits, to another various kinds of tongues, to another the interpretation of tongues. (12:8–10)

> God has appointed in the church first apostles, second prophets, third teachers, then miracles, then gifts of healing, helping, administrating, and various kinds of tongues. (12:28)

Understanding the gift lists as categories of people is not invalidated by the fact that some of those list entries are supernatural gifts. Clearly, as with all the gifts, some people in the early church had those supernatural gifts, and some did not. Thus, we are still dealing with people categories.

TO JOURNEY IS STILL THE NEED

If we are dealing with people categories, then we are dealing with individuals in the discovery, development, and use of their gifts, even when those are supernatural gifts. And as presented in this book, their journeys of growth are strategic for their realization and wise use of those gifts.

If someone's gifts include supernatural manifestations, such as healing or tongues, it may be that they involve God's direct initiation in ways that other gifts do not. To go deeper into that subject is beyond the scope of this book. [9] *But the importance of integrating gifting with growth is not set aside because some of the gifts involve a supernatural event that depends on God's initiation.*

Jesus seemed to think his disciples needed to mature in their faith in order to be his vessels for an exorcism (Matthew 17:14–21). And we've already seen that Paul felt the Corinthians, who were very active in powerful spiritual manifestations, had a huge need for spiritual growth to accompany those powers.

The reality that this is each person's need is underscored when we realize that a person with supernatural gifts will also have other gifted potentials that need development, and that all these potentials interact with one another in each unique person as a whole.

CONCLUDING THOUGHTS

Christians will probably always have disagreements about whether today God is acting miraculously through some of the *charismata*. But perhaps we can agree that all of the gifts are manifestations of the Spirit, whenever they have been or are seen.

If we adopt the Journey View of gifting, we shift our focus away from our disagreements to the potential we each have and the growth we each need in order to realize our potentials. It seems to me that a Christian, whether charismatic or noncharismatic, could embrace this Journey View. If Christians who hold differing views on the supernatural gifts could agree that the main scenes of gifting are our growth journeys and the battles in our hearts, it could contribute to unity in the greater body of Christ.

CONCLUSION

My deepest desire in publishing this book is not to introduce a different view of spiritual gifts. Years ago, that might have been my main desire. But then I spent years working with people to help them realize their true identity and potentials in Christ. It became clear to me that their journeys of healing and growth were the gifting journey I had discerned in Scripture. I saw that in my own journey as well.

I've felt too much joy and gratitude in watching people grow to make just sharing an alternative view of gifts my main reason for publishing this book. It is a fresh perspective on spiritual gifts, but only as a means to the end of knowing that people are fighting the heart battles, and retrieving the spoils, God has intended for them.

Those heart battles can be fought whether one adopts the Journey View or not. But if the church moved from a utilitarian understanding of gifts to a more substantive journey perspective of gifting, I believe that integration of gifting with growth could be a powerful motivation for people to fight the battles involved in becoming who God created each one to be.

My prayer is that God would bless each of us with a depth of *agape* with one another that links us together as strategic fellow journeyers, as we move closer and closer to the perfected grace-expressions of God that we each are. Together, we are his spectrum of grace.

WORKSHEET 1: AGAPE EVALUATION

In your study of the Journey View, you've learned that loving relationships are important for spiritual gifts to be developed and expressed by each person. God has designed the body of Christ to be the environment for those loving relationships. Your goal is to value and nurture each person's unique expression of God's grace. Review chapter 4 as a background for understanding and using this tool. Chapter 8 focuses on listening, which is also relevant as you evaluate your *agape*.

Since this tool is designed for use in small groups, it's also important to review the comments about types of groups in chapter 10, because that affects the usefulness of this worksheet for your group. Especially note there that some groups prioritize tasks over relationships, while others do the opposite.

A task-prioritized group is an important type of group in many situations, to meet a variety of needs. It can be a wonderful expression of love through serving. But a task group may find that going to the level of *agape* evaluated here may not fit with their goals. In-depth *agape* is challenging for a group or person. Your group will need to prioritize relationships over tasks in order to work toward the level of loving relationships described here.

The Agape Evaluation is based on the qualities of love listed in 1 Corinthians 13. In line with what you have studied in this book, it presents each quality through the lens of how loving relationships help one another discover and develop our unique potentials in our journeys of gifting. Therefore, I have divided our focus on *agape* into a receiving (Valuing) side and a giving (Nurturing) side with that goal in view. On the Nurturing side, love both affirms and challenges fellow journeyers.[1]

You may also use the Agape Evaluation individually, to assess where you are in your journey of learning to love. Simply substitute "I" and "my" in place of references to the group. I encourage you to do that. And whatever your strengths or weaknesses may be as you reflect on yourself and love, remember that we're all on a journey into better ways of sharing *agape*. It's not realistic to think any of us can score ten on all these qualities of love!

If you use this tool individually, I suggest you use each section to evaluate how you're doing at both giving and receiving the kind of *agape* described. Journaling your thoughts and feelings as you do this would be a constructive exercise.

To use this worksheet with a small group, I suggest that you first study together chapters 1 through 8 of this book and meet weekly for no less than thirteen weeks. You could certainly each study this worksheet before then and practice its applications of love in your group. But give your group at least thirteen weeks of getting to know one another before your group's evaluation discussion. I encourage group leaders to especially study "Fostering the Agape Environment" in chapter 10.

When the time is right for your group to use the Agape Evaluation, complete it individually at home and come to the next meeting to discuss your perceptions with each other. Of course, you don't know the truth about all these areas for every person in your group. But your group discussion is about the group in general, not specific members of the group. And you do have a sense of how your group is doing. As you read each statement, start it with "My sense is that . . ."

One reason that discussion needs to be delayed for at least thirteen weeks is that it involves honesty, vulnerability, and trust, and requires practicing love and respect while sharing and listening. The best way to share your perceptions is to make them about the group, not individuals, and to start with, "My experience is . . ." The best way to receive what others share is to accept it as their experience of the group, not of you individually. Practice good listening skills while you do this.

WORKSHEET EXPLANATION

You may want to make a copy of this worksheet to record your responses on, so you can reuse this master copy again in the future. You will evaluate your group (or yourself) in twelve areas of love that are mentioned in 1 Corinthians 13. For each area, you are asked to evaluate a statement about the Valuing side of love and the Nurturing side of love. *To evaluate each area, give your group (or yourself) a score from one to ten for each statement, with ten being the highest.*

The Valuing side of love is where we show that we *receive* the other person as they are. We communicate that we value each one as an individual, and that we value each person on God's spectrum of grace.

The Nurturing side of love is where we proactively *give* to one another the affirmations and challenges we all need. Love creates environments where we are nurtured to be people of hope and faith.

AGAPE EVALUATION AREAS

1. **Love Is Patient: 1 Corinthians 13:4**

    a. Valuing Love   Score:

    Each person in our group feels listened to or heard. We go beyond superficial impressions to more accurate understanding of each other.

    b. Nurturing Love   Score:

    We wait for the right times to share affirmation or challenge. And when we do, we make it fit that unique person's current need.

2. **Love Is Kind: 1 Corinthians 13:4**

    a. Valuing Love   Score:

    When someone's rough edges are showing, we are gentle. When someone is factually wrong, we don't rush to correct.

    b. Nurturing Love   Score:

    In affirming and challenging, our spirit is constructive, and our words are gentle.

3. **Love Does Not Envy (Is Not Jealous): 1 Corinthians 13:4**

   a. Valuing Love   Score:

   We notice and value the strengths of each other, not allowing envy to distort our perceptions.

   b. Nurturing Love   Score:

   Our affirmations and challenges truly serve the other person. They do not express our own selfish feelings about that person's strengths or weaknesses.

4. **Love Does Not Boast (Brag): 1 Corinthians 13:4**

   a. Valuing Love   Score:

   We do not evaluate certain kinds of personality or giftedness as better than others.

   b. Nurturing Love   Score:

   Our words of affirmation or challenge do not make us look better than another.

5. Love Is Not Arrogant (Proud): 1 Corinthians 13:4

a. Valuing Love   *Score:*

We view each other as persons we want to serve.

b. Nurturing Love   *Score:*

When we are affirming or challenging, we do not imply that the other person is less worthy or spiritual. We do not share a critical spirit.

6. Love Is Not Rude (Unbecoming): 1 Corinthians 13:5

a. Valuing Love   *Score:*

Each person in our group is received with respect and honor as someone made in God's image.

b. Nurturing Love   *Score:*

We give affirmation or challenge as an equal speaking to an equal.

7. **Love Is Not Self-Seeking (Insisting on Its Own Way):**
   1 Corinthians 13:5

   a. Valuing Love   Score:

   We welcome each person sharing their joys and pains. Our group is not controlled by the personal agenda of one or a few.

   b. Nurturing Love   Score:

   Personal gain is not sought in giving affirmation and challenge. Time, prayer, and effort go into it, for the other's good.

8. **Love Is Not Easily Angered (Not Provoked):**
   1 Corinthians 13:5

   a. Valuing Love   Score:

   When we feel criticized or poorly treated, we do not attack or become defensive.

   b. Nurturing Love   Score:

   When we give challenge, we do not do it in a spirit of getting back for something.

9. **Love Keeps No Record of Wrongs (Is Not Resentful): 1 Corinthians 13:5**

    a. Valuing Love   *Score:*

    We do not allow past wrongs to distort our acceptance of a person now.

    b. Nurturing Love   *Score:*

    When we give challenge, we do not communicate that a person must "pay" for wrongs done.

10. **Love Does Not Rejoice at Wrongdoing (or in Unrighteousness): 1 Corinthians 13:6**

    a. Valuing Love   *Score:*

    We feel authentically sad about sin in each other's lives.

    b. Nurturing Love   *Score:*

    When we know of sin in another, we allow our true grief to show, as a reflection of how God feels.

11. Love Rejoices with the Truth: 1 Corinthians 13:6

a Valuing Love   Score:

We feel true excitement when we see each other being authentic with God, others, and self.

b. Nurturing Love   Score:

We show excitement about cheering on the authentic development of another's unique potential.

12. Love Is Optimistic and Devoted (Bears, Believes, Hopes, Endures All Things): 1 Corinthians 13:7

a. Valuing Love   Score:

We have allowed God to place in our hearts a commitment to his vision for each person in our group.

b. Nurturing Love   Score:

We show steadfast support for each other's journeys toward full expression of potential, not bailing out because of each other's setbacks.

WORKSHEET 2: THE GIFTING JOURNEY

In the Journey View, spiritual gifts are defined as our God-given potentials that have been lost to (or damaged by) the effects of sin but can be progressively restored. So we "receive" (i.e., discover) our gifts during our journeys of growth.

Further, in *Spiritual Gifts Reimagined*, we have studied how the Old Testament process of Israel retrieving from enemies' hands the riches God intended for his people is a precedent for us to understand our own gifting journeys. As with Israel, our journeys involve following God into the battles we need to fight to gain spoils—our potentials that have been held hostage to sin and immaturity.

We have also seen that full restoration to all of our potentials is when we stand before Christ and receive from him our unique names (Revelation 2:17). That goal is pursued within the pursuit of becoming like Christ as we identify and carry our own crosses (Mark 8:34). Your developing uniqueness in displaying God grace is intertwined with your developing conformity to Christ.

These themes are developed earlier in this book. You'll want to review especially chapters 2, and 5 through 7, as background for using this worksheet. We saw in the example of Israel that the journey of retrieving spoils began with God's deliverance. Theirs was from Egypt, after which their gifting journey began. God delivers us from being lost without Christ. Then, with God's Spirit living in us, our journeys of discovering, developing, and using our potentials begin.[1]

Drawing on these themes, this worksheet gives you a tool for thinking about your gifting journey. In the Journey View, gifting is fully integrated with growing in Christ. Therefore, it involves identifying your potentials, the obstacles to developing them, the trials/battles God knows you need to experience in that development, and your proactive plans to engage with your gifting journey.

WORKSHEET EXPLANATION

You may want to make a copy of this worksheet to record your responses on. Then you can use copies of this master version repeatedly in the future.

Potentials / Spoils: You may or may not be aware of your potentials—the ones you have been living out and those that are still dormant within you. You were born with your gifts. Under Past, Present, and Future, record your best guesses as to the potentials, abilities, and strengths that are part of the unique you.

Obstacles / Enemies: Israel had to face their enemies to retrieve their riches, and so do we. Hebrews 12:1–2 says we must lay aside our encumbrances and sins to follow Christ. Your enemies are not other people or circumstances; they are your own sins and encumbrances. Ask God, and ask your close circle of trusted friends, to help you identify your obstacles to your growth and gifting.

Trials / Battles: God uses a spectrum of trials (James 1:2) to help each of us grow into being our unique hue on his spectrum of grace. Each trial involves a battle he invites us to fight in his strength. Look at your life's difficulties in this constructive way. They are the essential battles you must engage to keep growing into your full Christlike potential.

Proactive Steps: If you were to courageously engage in your battles, what specific steps would you take? What would you do today, tomorrow, next week and beyond to boldly cooperate with God's process in your journey? You'll have to face through fears and dive in. Discuss this with your closest friends, and trust God to use your courageous steps to restore you to who you uniquely are in Christ.

GIFTING JOURNEY AREAS

Your gifting journey begins with your personal deliverance when you receive salvation in Christ. It culminates when you attain Christlike uniqueness in his presence. In this worksheet (beginning on the next page) you'll explore the chronology of your gifting journey: its past, present, and future.

Past

1. Potentials / Spoils

What potentials did God seek to restore in your past?

2. Obstacles / Enemies (Encumbrances or Sins)

What have been your past obstacles to developing your unique potential?

3. Trials / Battles

Specify the past trials in which God was seeking to restore your unique potential.

4. Proactive Growth Steps

What steps did you take to cooperate with God's restoration?

Present

1. Potentials / Spoils

What are the potentials God is now seeking to restore in your life?

2. Obstacles / Enemies (Encumbrances or Sins)

Given the spoils God is now seeking to restore to you, what are your current obstacles?

3. Trials / Battles

Specify the current trials God is using to restore your unique potentials.

4. Proactive Growth Steps

Specify changes, new responsibilities, classes, accountabilities, counseling, spiritual disciplines, small groups, ministry service, and more—growth opportunities you can use to cooperate with God's restoration.

Future

1. Potentials / Spoils
What potentials might God want to restore in your future?

2. Obstacles / Enemies (Encumbrances or Sins)
What future enemies might you have to face as you let God restore your fortunes?

3. Trials / Battles
Anticipate future battles God may plan as you move toward full restoration.

4. Proactive Growth Steps
Specify changes, new responsibilities, classes, accountabilities, counseling, spiritual disciplines, small groups, ministry service (and more)—growth opportunities you can use to cooperate with God's restoration.

APPENDIX 1

PROPOSITIONAL SUMMARY

A PROPOSITIONAL SUMMARY OF THE METAPHORICAL (JOURNEY) VIEW OF SPIRITUAL GIFTS

The premise of *Spiritual Gifts Reimagined*, based on scriptural interpretations explained in this book, is that spiritual gifts are not about add-ons we get and use but rather the diversity of people we are.

The core theme of *Spiritual Gifts Reimagined* is that spiritual gifts must be integrated with spiritual growth.

The following propositions relate to this premise and theme:

1. Spiritual gifting is a metaphor in the Epistles—alongside the accompanying metaphor of the church as the body of Christ. Neither is intended to be understood in a concrete way (reified). Treating gifts as things we get (added to us) has led to a mechanistic understanding of spiritual gifting.

2. The list entries in the New Testament gift passages are category headings, conceived by Paul and Peter as they observed the diverse body of Christ, and presented flexibly several times in their teachings. The data in the categories are people, not

gifts per se. Use of some gifts involves supernatural initiation, but does not set aside the idea that the lists contain people categories. As inspired scripture, the lists describe healthy church functioning.

3. Definition of spiritual gifts: Spiritual gifts are our God-given potentials that have been lost to (or damaged by) the effects of sin but can be progressively restored. So we "receive" (i.e., discover and develop) our gifts during our journeys of growth. Complete restoration to unique giftedness is when we stand before Christ and each receive our unique new name.

4. Therefore, spiritual gifts are not entities that are automatically received by people at specific points in time. We are born with these potentials, yet they await the indwelling and power of the Holy Spirit to be developed in God-honoring ways.

5. As such, unbelievers have gifts from God. Their giftings are wonderful and often on display. Due to the lack of the Spirit of God in their lives, however, their use of their gifts may be inconsistent with God's purposes (which we Christians also struggle with).

6. There is no necessary distinction between spiritual gifts and natural talents. All are God-sourced. We are whole persons, not divided into spiritual and natural.

7. The discovery, development, and use of a person's gifts are necessarily intertwined with, and dependent upon, that person's ongoing spiritual growth as a disciple following Jesus Christ. That growth could also be called psychospiritual, involving the whole person and many different aspects of personal development, maturation, and education.

APPENDIX 2

THE SPOILS THEME

Beginning in chapter 2, we learned that the apostle Paul believed that gifting was seen before, in Israel's journey from Egypt into the promised land. He prompts us to connect that Old Testament journey of God's people to spiritual gifts in Ephesians 4:8. He cites Psalm 68:18, where gifts are spoils of the many battles God has led his people in through the preceding centuries.

In the psalm, David pictures God the King receiving those spoils from vanquished enemies, then gifting his people with the spoils. Of course, the victories that garnered those spoils required God's people to faithfully follow him into many battles. God responded to their faithfulness by giving them victories and enriching them with the spoils as gifts.

This is the journey of gifting: faithfully engaging with the battles God has in your path of growth, and greater and greater experience of the inheritance (promised land) he has for you. The Old Testament stories of battles, the times God's people were faithful to engage those battles, and the times they were not—and what it was like to experience all that—are inspiration for us to engage our battles and follow the Lord for our growth and gifting.

There is not space in this book to explore these many references. I encourage you to use the scriptures below to study the Old Testament motif of spoils. After listing them, I will share some relevant hermeneutical considerations.

SPOILS IN OT SCRIPTURES

First, there are scripture passages that show us the historical flow of spoils-as-gifts in the journey of God's people. Most of these are references to spoils of specific battles or victories. Some are broader references to the taking of Canaan as their inheritance.

Spoils Related to Exodus from Egypt
Genesis 15:13–14
Exodus 3:20–22
Exodus 12:35–36

Spoils on the Journey from Egypt to Canaan
Numbers 21:21–25, 33–35
Deuteronomy 2:30–3:8
Psalm 135:10–12
Psalm 136:17–22

Spoils During Conquest of the Promised Land
Numbers 33:50–54
Numbers 34:2
Deuteronomy 3:20–22
Deuteronomy 6:10–11

Second, there are scriptures that indicate to us in various ways the importance of the theme of spoils in God's ways of working with his people.

The Importance of Israel's Plundering of Their Enemies
Numbers 31
Deuteronomy 20:13–16
Joshua 8:2, 27
Joshua 11:10–23
Joshua 22:7–9
2 Samuel 8:3–4, 7–12
2 Samuel 12:29–30
1 Chronicles 20:1–2
1 Chronicles 26:26–27
2 Chronicles 14:12–15
2 Chronicles 20:22–25
Esther 8:11
Zephaniah 2:9

The Theme of God's People Being Despoiled by Enemies
This theme highlights for us the true-to-life, give-and-take of battles. When Israel failed to engage with the battles God wanted them to fight, they not only forfeited or postponed riches he intended for them, but they also opened themselves up to being plundered—despoiled—by their enemies. If we are not moving forward—through our battles, in our journeys of gifting—the enemies of our hearts are pulling us backward, further away from realizing our rich potentials.

Despoiling of Israel Imagined
Exodus 15:9
Numbers 14:3, 31 (NIV)
Judges 5:19, 30
Esther 3:13

Despoiling of Israel Recorded
2 Chronicles 24:23

Despoiling of Israel Contemplated
Isaiah 42:22–25
Jeremiah 2:14 (NIV)
Ezekiel 23:46
Ezekiel 36:2-5 (NIV)
Ezekiel 38:10–13

Despoiling of Israel Prophesied
Jeremiah 15:13–14
Jeremiah 17:3–4
Jeremiah 20:5
Ezekiel 7:21–24

The Idea That Israel Will Plunder Enemies Who Previously Plundered Them

Isaiah 49:24–25 (NIV)
Jeremiah 30:16
Ezekiel 39:10
Zechariah 14:1–3, 14

Cross reference the similar principle in Proverbs 22:23 (NIV).

Prophecies and Prayers That God Will Despoil Israel's Enemies
Nehemiah 4:4
Psalm 109:11
Isaiah 8:4
Isaiah 10:6
Isaiah 11:14
Isaiah 33:4, 23 (NIV)
Jeremiah 49:29, 32
Jeremiah 50:10
Ezekiel 25:4, 7
Ezekiel 26:5, 12
Ezekiel 29:19
Nahum 2:9

Third, David may be a Messianic type of gift (spoils) distribution in 1 Samuel 30.

Fourth, in words written for God's people to read once they'd been exiled to enemy lands due to their unfaithfulness to God, there is a parallel to the spoils theme: the common prophetic phrase "I will restore your fortunes."

Although the exile of God's people at the hands of their enemies seemed to deal a death blow to their inheritance of the promised land, God promises to restore them to the enrichment with spoils they previously tasted. As we saw in chapter 2, this encourages us that our failures are not the final word. When you get off track in your journey of growing into the gifted you God intended, his promise to you is . . . "I will restore your fortunes."

The English Standard Version (ESV) and the New International Version (NIV) Occurrences of Restoring Fortunes

Deuteronomy 30:3
Psalm 14:7
Psalm 53:6
Psalm 126:4

The English Standard Version (ESV) and the New American Standard Version (NASB) Occurrences of Restoring Fortunes

Jeremiah 29:14
Jeremiah 30:3, 18
Jeremiah 31:23
Jeremiah 32:44
Jeremiah 33:7, 11, 26
Ezekiel 39:25
Hosea 6:11
Joel 3:1
Zephaniah 2:7
Zephaniah 3:20

Conclusion: God's process of blessing his covenant people involves gradually taking out of enemy hands the riches he intended for his people. As he wins those battles, he puts into our hands the spoils as gifts (cf. Psalms 68:7–18 and 105:37–44).

HERMENEUTICAL NOTES

The use of the Old Testament in the New Testament is an area of considerable scholarly debate. The purpose and scope of this book do not allow me to fully treat that subject here as it applies to Paul's use of Psalm 68:18. But the questions in that area relate to the original meaning of the psalmist, the hermeneutics of the apostle, the change in words he makes, progressive revelation, etc.

I believe most studies of spiritual gifts have neglected the significance of the Ephesians 4:8 citation, and that an appropriate study of it yields wisdom concerning our gifts, developed in this book under the heading "spoils journey." The metanarrative Paul points to becomes a background that brings real-life texture to the integration of gifting with growth already implicit in his Epistles.

In this book I am suggesting that we replace the popular spiritual gift doctrine that says reception of our gifts happens when we receive the Holy Spirit (usually considered conversion) and is unrelated to our developmental status and our natural talents. In its place I am setting forth a doctrine that says we are born with our gifts and their discovery, development, and use are fully integrated with and dependent on our growth.

To summarize, spiritual growth is contextually connected with spiritual gifts in all of Paul's letters that mention gifts. And the spoils motif he points to illustrates and corroborates this developmental journey understanding of gifting.

I mentioned in chapter 12 that the direct scriptural teachings on gifts are limited. The question is whether you will fill our resulting vacuum of understanding about gifts with a mechanical idea that sees gifting as a point-in-time event based on a few verses in 1

Corinthians 12, or whether you'll allow contextual studies and the canonical connections of the gift passages to form a foundation for an understanding that integrates gifts with growth.

Two other matters deserve mention related to using the gifts-as-spoils metaphor. One relates to the interpretation of Ephesians 4:8–10 to illuminate our thinking about gifting. I briefly treated this matter toward the end of chapter 14 (and in its endnotes). Related to the spoils theme, I want to comment on how interpreting 4:9–10 as a reference to Christ's incarnation and ascension fits with that applied theme.

In that interpretation, these two verses (4:9–10) are strongly telling us to focus on Christ when we think about gifts, because they exclusively focus on his descent and ascent (rather than the Spirit's descent).[1] As such they form part of why I believe we need a Christocentric, rather than a Spirit-centered, theology of gifts. I developed that theme elsewhere, especially where we touched on cross wisdom.

But the relevance, for the spoils journey metaphor introduced in 4:8, of interpreting the descent in Ephesians 4:9–10 as Christ's incarnation is that Christ has walked that journey ahead of us. He fought the battles he had to fight. As God the King did for his people, poetically reprised in Psalm 68, Jesus came down and involved himself in the mud and grime of real battles (see chapter 7), becoming our ascending Victor who invites us to follow him through our battles.

Finally, I'll share a comment with those of you who teach and preach Scripture to others. In chapter 9, I encouraged you to fill our minds with the metanarrative that invites us to find our journeys in biblical story. We need the encouragement to fight our battles in the gifting journey, and their precedents are in the battle stories and spoils descriptions in the scriptures listed in this appendix.

However, the study necessary to do a responsible job of narrative exposition is such that many preachers and teachers avoid it and simply present what appears to them on the surface of a biblical story. As I encourage you to teach and preach the biblical metanarrative of spiritual gifts as spoils of battles, I exhort you, and myself, to apply sound hermeneutics in dealing with the narratives and other Old Testament literary forms that reveal the spoils motif.[2]

See chapter 14 for more specific discussions of Paul's use of Psalm 68 in Ephesians 4.

APPENDIX 3

INTEGRATION ISSUES

INTEGRATION AROUND CATEGORIES

Popular view proponents often add other (extra-biblical) categories alongside gifts to help people further narrow down an understanding of their specific or unique potentials. When they do this, they are, perhaps without realizing it, using a particular philosophy of interdisciplinary integration.[1]

Thomistic integration tends to segregate the sacred from the secular, while seeing value in what studies from disciplines in each area contribute. Gift studies that add extra-biblical categories to provide a fuller understanding of a person's uniqueness are an example of this. The reason this becomes a Thomistic approach is because these studies start with a reified understanding of gifts, which segregates spiritual gifts from the other human dimensions that are added.[2]

Instead of teaching that spiritual gifts are one aspect of you and that natural talents, skills, personality, passion, and so on are other parts of you, the Journey (Metaphorical) View sees gift categories and extra-biblical categories as various lenses through which we understand whole persons.

The popular view's Thomistic integration has not been without value for people seeking to clarify their unique gifting. But in an

Augustinian style of integration, spiritual gifts are not intending to describe only one specialized dimension of the human person that leaves out other dimensions (even though the biblical categories are chosen for the distinct purpose of church application). Instead, we see the biblical input as describing gifted whole persons, we give that input priority, and we welcome insights from other disciplines if it is consistent with biblical insights.

This is an Augustinian approach because it does not segregate persons into spiritual and natural parts, while using wisdom from both biblical gift categories and extra-biblical categories. The latter can be useful, but their (Thomistic) use in the popular view seems to imply the inadequacy of the biblical gift categories. Since the popular view rests on a reification of the concept of spiritual gifts, it ends up with this questionable style of integration.

If you instead begin with an understanding of spiritual gifting as metaphorical, you are able to see the gift lists as a particular biblical grid for understanding human diversity, unique individuals, whole persons. You are able to use other extra-biblical categories as well without implying the inadequacy of the biblical categories.

INTEGRATION AROUND DEVELOPMENT

As emphasized in this book, the Journey View integrates gifting with growth. I've mentioned that popular view authors often neglect the importance of maturing for gift development. Those who talk about the importance of growth do not truly integrate gifting with growth. This lack of integration, like the lack in the previous area, stems from the reification of gifts as a starting point.

Most people instinctively understand that discovery, development, and use of one's potentials depends upon multifaceted personal growth. The popular view's idea that new abilities automatically appear in the midst of a person's developmental journey seems out of sync with this common understanding. That is especially the case when you add the idea, frequently taught in the popular view, that your spiritual gifts are different than your natural talents.

Of course, there has been extensive research in the field of human development, and sometimes insights from developmental psychology echo biblical understandings. Those insights often reinforce our instinctive awareness that use of our potentials increases as we make progress in our developmental journeys. This corresponds with biblical implications about the importance of spiritual growth for our abilities to minister to others in wise and godly ways.

Integration around both categories and development are aspects of an interdisciplinary integration of spirituality or theology with psychology. That is a broad field and others have the credentials to speak to it. My desire is to point out that the biblical topic of spiritual gifts calls for thoughtful interdisciplinary integration and should be part of a solid biblical anthropology.

ENDNOTES

Introduction

1   In thinking about spiritual gifts, we can focus on the individual gifts and how they make each person distinctive, or we can focus on what is involved in being spiritually gifted that is common to us all. Doing both well in one book would be difficult. The popular view has largely emphasized the individual gifts and overlooked important biblical themes relevant in the spiritual gifting of all of us. The two emphases are interrelated, but this book, instead of listing and defining individual gifts, focuses on biblical themes that are essential as a context for understanding and experiencing differentiated spiritual gifting.
2   Grant R. Osborne, *The Hermeneutical Spiral: A Comprehensive Introduction to Interpretation* (Downers Grove, IL: InterVarsity Press, 1991), 316.
3   Osborne, *The Hermeneutical Spiral*, 300. Osborne writes that it is the "dissimilarity" of the metaphorical image, with perceived reality, "that leads the reader to rethink definitions."

Chapter One: Spectrum of Grace

1   1 Peter 4:10. United Bible Societies, *The Greek New Testament*, 3d ed., Kurt Aland, Matthew Black, Carlo M. Martini, Bruce M. Metzger, and Allen Wikgren (New York: American Bible Society, 1975), 800. The form of the adjective in 1 Peter 4:10 is *poikilēs* since it modifies *charitos*, but I will use the basic masculine form throughout, which is how it appears in lexicons as the main entry.
2   G. Abbott-Smith, *A Manual Greek Lexicon of the New Testament* (Edinburgh: T. & T. Clark, 1968), 369–370. "Poikilos," Eulexis-web, Baobab, accessed November 2, 2021, https://outils.biblissima.fr/fr/eulexis-web/?lemma=%CF%80%CE%BF%CE%B9%CE%BA%CE%B9%CE%BB%CE%BF%CF%82&dict=LSJ. The use of *poikilos* ranged beyond art to sometimes simply mean diversity or complexity in any area. See also James Hope Moulton and George Milligan, *The*

227

Vocabulary of the Greek Testament: Illustrated from the Papyri and other Non-Literary Sources, rev. ed.(1930, Grand Rapids, MI: Eerdmans, 1982), 523.
3   Christopher S. Baird, "Why are there only six fundamental colors: red, orange, yellow, green, blue, and violet?" Science Questions with Surprising Answers, accessed November 3, 2021, https://www.wtamu.edu/~cbaird/sq/2012/12/04/why-are-there-only-six-fundamental-colors-red-orange-yellow-green-blue-and-violet/.
4   Abbott-Smith, *Greek Lexicon*, 369–371. As seen in the lexical entries for *poikilos* and *polupoikilos*, as well as in other instances of the use of this preposition, *polu* has an intensifying effect on the word's idea.
5   Eugene Peterson, *Working the Angles: The Shape of Pastoral Integrity* (Grand Rapids, MI: Eerdmans, 1987), 127.

Chapter Two: The Spoils Journey

1   Derek Kidner, *Tyndale Old Testament Commentaries*, ed. D. J. Wiseman, vol. 14a, *Psalms 1–72: An Introduction and Commentary* (Downers Grove, IL: InterVarsity Press, 1973), 238.
2   Especially in the quote from Moses in 68:1 (cf. Numbers 10:35), but also in the designation of God as "the One of Sinai" (68:8). It recalls their meeting with him after their deliverance from and spoiling of the Egyptians. Note also in 68:6 where God "leads out the prisoners."
3   Kidner, *Tyndale Old Testament Commentaries*, 14a:238–241. I will not go through the psalm verse by verse, but Kidner clarifies how the poetry of the psalm (particularly in 68:1-14) rehearses Israel's journey from Egypt through the wilderness and into the promised land. Leopold Sabourin, *The Psalms: Their Origin and Meaning* (New York: Alba House, 1974), 328. Sabourin indicates that the "main phases of *Heilsgeschichte* (salvation history) are celebrated in this triumphal hymn . . ." For our purposes, the point is that Psalm 68 is an overview of how God has worked with his people in their history that he has superintended. That "salvation history" includes dominant themes like deliverance, covenant, and inheritance. God's ascent, and the gifts that flow to his people through his hands, form the climax of that history in this psalm and is pointed to by Paul as precedent for spiritual gifting, now fulfilled through Christ's victorious ascent.
4   Kidner, *Tyndale Old Testament Commentaries*, 14a:242. Tremper Longman III and Daniel G. Reid, *God is a Warrior*, Studies in Old Testament Biblical Theology, eds. Willem A. VanGemeren and

ENDNOTES

Tremper Longman III (Grand Rapids, MI: Zondervan Publishing House, Kindle edition, 1995), 35-36. Longman and Reid comment of the ark: "From its description in Exodus, it sounds most like the footstool to God's throne."

5 C. F. Keil and F. Delitzsch, *Commentary on the Old Testament*, translated by Francis Bolton, vol. 5:2, *Psalms*, by F. Delitzsch (Grand Rapids, MI: Eerdmans, 1975, original edition, 1871), 261–262. Delitzsch refers to the Ephesians 4:8 gift-giving: "It is a distribution of gifts, a dispensing of blessing, which stands related to His victory as its primary cause; for as Victor He is also the possessor of blessing. His gifts are as it were the spoils of victory He has gained over sin, death, and Satan."

6 I am leaving comment on Ephesians 4:9–10 for later (toward the end of chapter 14) because it is not strategic here to the main point that gifting has been seen before, in the spoils journey of Israel. See also my comments on these two verses toward the end of appendix 2.

7 D. Moody Smith, "The Pauline literature," in *It Is Written: Scripture Citing Scripture: Essays in Honour of Barnabas Lindars*, ed. D. A. Carson and H. G. M. Williamson (Cambridge: University Press, 1988), 281. In this quote, Smith is translating Swiss theologian Ulrich Luz.

8 C. S. Lewis, The Chronicles of Narnia, vol. 2, *The Lion, the Witch and the Wardrobe* (New York: HarperCollins, 1950).

9 In this chapter I am presenting the spoils theme Paul points to as an illustration of gifting by our ascending Christ. In calling it an illustration, I am clarifying that I do not base the Journey View's integration of gifting with growth on this Psalm 68 citation. As I will clarify in part 4, the basis of that integration is the emphasis on growth in the spiritual gift contexts of the Epistles in tandem with the interpretation that gifting is metaphorical. I believe Paul's contribution of this spoils illustration is corroborative to those foundational perspectives.

10 I will later develop the idea that we are born with our gifts/potentials. To say we receive our gifts along the journey is to express the idea in terms of the spoils metaphor we are discussing here. This reception literally refers to discovery and/or development of our gifted potentials.

11 Dan B. Allender, *To Be Told: God Invites You to Coauthor Your Future* (Colorado Springs, CO: WaterBrook Press, 2005), 46.

Chapter Three: Cross Wisdom

1   Sam Storms, *Understanding Spiritual Gifts* (Grand Rapids, MI: Zondervan, Kindle edition, 2020), 12–16. Sam Storms helpfully explains and applies how the multi-membered body of Christ gives value to each member so that we need one another. His comments are based on 1 Corinthians 12. While he does not relate them to the wisdom of the cross in 1 Corinthians 1, that theme is felt in his words, especially when he discusses those who feel more important than other members.

2   Our doctrine of spiritual gifts should be built upon broader biblical doctrines. Therefore, as we discern and pursue the canonical connections of spiritual gifts, we are tracing a path backwards to foundational truths. Thus, body wisdom is based on cross wisdom, not the reverse. In chapter 7 we will discern another dimension of cross wisdom that is also foundational for our understanding of spiritual gifts.

3   Howard A. Snyder, *The Problem of Wineskins: Church Structure in a Technological Age* (Downers Grove, IL: InterVarsity Press, 1975), 135–136. In the 1970s, Howard Snyder, in critiquing the church's thinking about spiritual gifts, listed one of the problems as "[t]he tendency to divorce spiritual gifts from the cross." He does not develop the connection between 1 Corinthians 1 and 12 but does helpfully focus on the psychospiritual dynamics involved in adopting what I call here cross wisdom and their impact on gift development and expression. We will be looking more at that in chapter 7 as we study how Christ challenges us to carry our crosses, which Snyder also relates to being spiritually gifted.

4   Paul R. Ford, *Unleash Your Church! A Comprehensive Strategy to Help People Discover and Use their Spiritual Gifts* (Pasadena, CA: Charles E. Fuller Institute, 1993), 24–25, cf. 44, 57–58. This proponent of the popular view of gifts, Paul Ford, stresses that the "corporate life" of God's people "is not primarily an organization but rather an organism called the body of Christ." He sees organizational roles as secondary to spiritual gifts, which arise from the church's organismic identity.

5   Today, it is tempting for us, as Christians, to draw back from making such affirmations. That is because the world has taken the idea of being your authentic self and twisted it into meanings that stray beyond the wisdom and grace of God. One way you can spot the misuse of this idea is by noticing that the world's form of

"authenticity" is often just conformity to (imitation within) new categories it has come up with, not a true discerning of your unique identity. See chapter 11 for further thoughts on this.
6   C. S. Lewis, *The Weight of Glory: And Other Addresses* (New York: Macmillan Publishing, 1949), 18.

Chapter Four: Powerful Love

1   Larry J. Crabb, *Connecting: Healing for Ourselves and Our Relationships, a Radical New Vision* (Nashville, TN: Word, 1997), 52. Larry Crabb's insights about the power of authentic relationships fit perfectly with the focus of this chapter. He writes, "Powerful relating consists in grasping a vision of what God has in mind for someone and the faith to believe that the vision could become reality. A godly vision generates an excruciating sorrow when someone moves away from that vision, but that sorrow never eliminates hope or leads to disdain. And a godly vision releases giddy excitement when someone moves toward it, even just a little." Larry Crabb, *Soul Talk: The Language God Longs for Us to Speak* (Brentwood, TN: Integrity Publishers, 2003), 201. In this later book he writes, "Looking bad in the presence of love releases our true self."
2   Roberta Hestenes, *Building Christian Community Through Small Groups* (Pasadena, CA: Fuller Seminary Bookstore, 1985), 38. "The discovery and use of spiritual gifts takes place in contexts that are personal rather than impersonal. I do not discover my ministry by looking in the mirror or by contemplating my navel. I discover who I am and what I am called to do in the context of significant relationships with other people."
3   Crabb, *Soul Talk*. Crabb doggedly pursues and bluntly confronts us with the need for these deeper connections as fellow journeyers. He exposes our preference for the easy path of offering sympathy and empathy, teaching how truth working in love in relationships can connect each of us with God's deeper purposes for our growth.
4   Allender, *To Be Told*, 93. "We simply can't see our own face. If we want to know the truth about ourselves, we must be in relational dialogue. That's how God made us."
5   D. A. Carson, *Showing the Spirit: A Theological Exposition of 1 Corinthians 12–14* (Grand Rapids, MI: Baker Book House, 1987), 23. Carson affirms that Paul introduces his gifts teaching in 1 Corinthians 12 by using "the terms preferred by his Corinthian

readers . . . and that at least through chapter 12 he then proceeds to use the term he himself prefers . . ." He is referring to the switch from *pneumatikon* to *charisma*, and states that this "serves to lay emphasis on grace" as the "source of all true spiritual gifts."
6   Note that, in the Agape Evaluation worksheet, a small group is advised not to use the tool as a group until they have met together for at least thirteen weeks.
7   Crabb, *Connecting*, 52.

Chapter Five: Imagine Your Inheritance
1   David G. Benner, *Psychotherapy and the Spiritual Quest* (Grand Rapids, MI: Baker, 1988), 41, 52. I use the term "psychospiritual" in the way suggested by David Benner, to refer to sanctification (Christian maturing) as "becoming whole." He believes "we need . . . a broadened view of spirituality and a way of intimately relating it to and placing it within the overall framework of psychospiritual functions and processes of personality." Benner's holistic understanding comports with the view presented here that spiritual gifts are integrated with a person's identity and developmental journey.
2   In chapter 14 we will discuss interpretation of these verses at a more detailed level.
3   Brent Curtis and John Eldredge, *The Sacred Romance: Drawing Closer to the Heart of God* (Nashville, TN: Thomas Nelson, Inc., 1997), 44–45.

Chapter Six: Engage Your Battles
1   David G. Benner, *Psychotherapy and the Spiritual Quest* (Grand Rapids, MI: Baker, 1988). The term is suggested by David Benner. See my endnote on its meaning in the last chapter, along with Benner's comments.
2   C. S. Lewis, *The Screwtape Letters* (New York: Macmillan, 1942, reprint 1961), xii (page reference is to the preface to the paperback edition).
3   Allender, *To Be Told*, 30, 51–52. Allender mines the meaning for our lives of our white stone names.
4   We will consider further, in chapter 7, the relevance of our true and false selves in our journeys' battles.
5   Lewis, *The Weight of Glory*, 6–7.
6   Warren J. Heard, Jr., "Eschatologically Oriented Psychology: A New

Paradigm for the Integration of Psychology and Christianity," in *God and Culture: Essays in Honor of Carl F. H. Henry*, ed. D. A. Carson and John D. Woodbridge (Grand Rapids, MI: William B. Eerdmans Publishing, 1993), 106–133. Warren Heard argues that a scriptural understanding of history and use of the Christ-event as a proleptic lens for discerning what is true leads to an "eschatologically oriented psychology." His desire is that people would perceive their future wholeness in Christ, which the Spirit can use as a grounding anchor. This future-oriented perspective is what I am pointing to as we think about our new names.
7   Allender, *To Be Told*, 16.

Chapter Seven: Be You Like Christ

1   Wordspring Music LLC, Meaux Jeaux Music, Da Bears Da Bears Da Bears Music, Tony Wood Songs.
2   Among the classic examples is C. Peter Wagner, *Your Spiritual Gifts Can Help Your Church Grow* (Ventura, CA: Regal Books, 1979), 13. A more recent example is Sam Storms, *The Beginner's Guide to Spiritual Gifts* (Bloomington, MN: Bethany House Publishers, 2012), 8–9. Some books on gifts briefly reference Christ, but not in a way central to their treatment of gifts. Examples are Bruce Bugbee, Don Cousins, and Bill Hybels, *Network: The Right People in the Right Places for the Right Reasons—Leader's Guide* (Grand Rapids, MI: Zondervan, 1994), 108, 234; Ford, *Unleash Your Church!* 170.
3   D. A. Carson, Notes by Bill Smart in Carson's class "Hermeneutics and Homiletics" (June 8–11, 1992), 3. According to D. A. Carson, scriptural exposition at its best draws attention to the "canonical connections that inexorably move toward Jesus Christ." It seems to me that many books on spiritual gifts actually are not attempting to do scriptural exposition. They have an applied focus, which is appropriate, but have made assumptions about how the scriptures about gifts are to be interpreted. I will say more about the importance of "canonical connections," for our understanding of the gift passages, in chapter 13. Outside of that chapter, I am often using phrases like "biblical threads" in place of "canonical connections."
4   As we look at Jesus in the context of this study on spiritual gifts, we focus on his example (cross-carrying) and his call to follow his example (echoed in Hebrews 12:1–2). This is not to replace

the foundational reality that Jesus' death on the cross is first our atonement for sins, but that is not the focus of our present study.

5   I encourage you to think about what a statement of your life's mission would say. It's not a mechanical process and not superficial or quickly discerned. My mission statement came in a kind of epiphany moment, yet in hindsight I realized it was the fruit of years of development and marinating in the values that are truest in my heart. It also raised a few eyebrows. Jesus' mission raised questions and challenges, didn't it? Even he struggled with his mission, in Gethsemane (Luke 22:39–46). See Allender's wisdom on discerning your mission statement. Allender, *To Be Told*, 119–122.

6   See Mark 8:34–38. Jesus clarifies that his invitation to deny self and carry one's cross calls you to make a choice: save your life or lose it. We give in to the pressure to conform to others' expectations because we want to have a life and we think that's the way. We're deceived, Jesus says. Following Jesus in denying that false self and carrying one's cross is the way to life.

7   Gary W. Moon, *Homesick for Eden: A Soul's Journey to Joy* (Ann Arbor, MI: Servant Publications, 1997), 43–47, 192–194, 271. Christian authors and teachers frequently use the concepts of true and false selves to describe the struggles in the Christian journey. Moon also lists psychologists (including Christians) who have used these concepts.

8   Lewis, *Weight of Glory*, 3. "The New Testament has lots to say about self-denial, but not about self-denial as an end in itself." Lewis goes on to emphasize reward but makes a similar point to mine: self-denial is in the service of other goals.

9   Thomas Merton, "Learning to Live," in *Love and Living*, ed. Naomi Burton Stone and Patrick Hart (Orlando, FL: Harcourt Brace, 1979), 3. Merton wrote: "Life consists in learning to live on one's own, spontaneous, freewheeling: to do this one must recognize what is one's own—be familiar and at home with oneself. This means basically learning who one is, and learning what one has to offer to the contemporary world, and then learning how to make this offering valid."

10 Eric Metaxas, *Bonhoeffer: Pastor, Martyr, Prophet, Spy* (Nashville, TN: Thomas Nelson, 2010). My wife and I recently read this biography of Dietrich Bonhoeffer. He is an excellent modern example of a Christian who discerned his unique mission as a Christ follower,

a mission which arose out of his unique identity, and accepted in advance the sacrifices that mission would, and did, involve.
11 David G. Benner, *The Gift of Being Yourself: The Sacred Call to Self-Discovery* (Expanded Edition) (Downers Grove, IL: InterVarsity Press, (Kindle Edition) 2015), 17, 73-74, 93-94. Benner extensively analyzes the psychospiritual journey of becoming you like Christ. He emphasizes that growing into Christlikeness involves becoming your true self, the importance of clarity about your false self in that process, how that identity formation flows into unique mission, and how Christ is our example in this process.
12 Of course, Christ was primarily motivated by love, as Scripture makes clear. Here I am emphasizing, however, what is focused on in this Hebrews passage. And that observation would apply also to the applications for ourselves from Christ's example.
13 The whole Epistle to the Hebrews climaxes with the escalating challenges and reminders in 10:19 through 12:29. The readers are exhorted to endure in following Christ, and the emphases are in sync with Christ's call to carry our crosses.
14 Peterson, *Working the Angles*, 113.

Chapter Eight: Your Listening Community
1 Wagner, *Your Spiritual Gifts Can Help Your Church Grow*, 52. Wagner wrote, "Spiritual gifts are utilitarian. They are functional." Bruce Bugbee, Don Cousins, and Bill Hybels, *Network: The Right People in the Right Places for the Right Reasons—Participant's Guide* (Grand Rapids, MI: Zondervan, 1994), 139. Bugbee concurs: "Fruit of the Spirit . . . is a 'be' quality, while Spiritual Gifts are 'do' qualities." Storms, *Understanding Spiritual Gifts*, xvi, 31. A more recent example of this dichotomy between task and being is Sam Storms, who sees the Spirit's fruit as more important than his gifts: "Character is always more important than gifting. Said another way, who we are now and are becoming by virtue of God's sanctifying influence in our hearts is more vital to the individual and to the corporate experience of God's people than what we do." And elsewhere, "Spiritual gifts are concrete manifestations of the Spirit through us. They are not who we are, therefore, but rather what we do in the power of the Spirit for the good of others."
2 Crabb, *Soul Talk*, 139. This fascination is similar to what Crabb refers to as "transcendent curiosity," which focuses on the deeper story of, and

where God is working in, a person's life. "We must lead with our ears into the particular story of someone's life. Curiosity begins the process."
3   I received training in healthy speaking and listening from Interpersonal Communication Programs, Inc. (ICP) and have taught the skills to others. My brief comments on how to listen are based on that training. ICP training is now available through Tyro Support Services. You can learn more at tyro365.com.
4   Sherod Miller and Phyllis Miller, *Core Communication: Maps, Skills, and Processes* (Evergreen, CO: Interpersonal Communication Programs, Inc., 2011), 51–58, 103.
5   Miller and Miller, *Core Communication*, 102.
6   Miller and Miller, *Core Communication*, 108–110.
7   Crabb, *Soul Talk*, 188.

Chapter Nine: Values for Church—Teaching and Growth

1   Our greatest fulfillment is in knowing, glorifying, and enjoying the Lord. Indeed, through our spiritual gifting and growth into our gifting, we grow in our knowing, glorifying, and enjoying him. Within that, however, when we consider the Scripture's teachings concerning the varied gifting of each person, and in the context of a biblical doctrine of the dignity of image-bearing humans, we find that we are each invited to the fulfillment of becoming our true unique selves in Christ.
2   As in Ephesians 4:3–16, Romans 12:4–6, and 1 Corinthians 12:4–6, 11–14.
3   In other words, the idea of diversely gifted people is not fundamentally utilitarian. Fundamentally, it is referring to the diversity of people that we are in our being. Certainly, that diversity of being flows into diversity of functioning, as reflected in the gift lists and their contexts. But I believe that Paul's emphasis falls more on unity in diversity (relational and attitudinal) than on roles and functions. The latter are secondary; the former are primary.
4   Ephesians 4:15–16; Colossians 3:14–15; 1 Corinthians 12:12–13; 1 Peter 2:4–5.
5   The commonalities I'm thinking of here are a) having our identities in our new lives in Christ, b) our condition of having been rescued from life without Christ, and c) being on the journey of moving from our false selves toward our true selves and fighting the battles to recover our potentials that have been held hostage to sin.

6 Allender, *To Be Told*, 46.
7 Lewis, The Chronicles of Narnia, vol. 2, *The Lion, the Witch and the Wardrobe*.
8 Wagner, *Your Spiritual Gifts Can Help Your Church Grow*, 224. Wagner writes, "The ability to discover spiritual gifts . . . is a function of emotional maturity." Ford, *Unleash Your Church!*, 37, 43, 102, 256. Ford seems to see maturation as not optional for a Christian wanting to develop giftedness, but he does not thoroughly integrate the two. Ronald B. Oertli, *Right Fit: Discover Who You Are and Where You Fit* (Littleton, CO: Stepstones, 1996), 15, 33–35, 172. Oertli, developer of the Navigators 2:7 material, does stress, more than other authors, specifics of discipleship in his teaching about gifts. But like the others, he seems to be connecting two separate biblical themes rather than seeing them as completely integrated. Though popular books about gifts vary in their mentions of the importance of growth, their teachings have not led the average Christian to significantly associate gifts with growth.
9 Perhaps this sounds like a harsh critique. But mention of Jesus is minimal in most publications about gifts. Some may mention Jesus' example of being a servant and may opine that he probably had all the gifts. As developed here, Jesus is the ultimate paragon for understanding what is involved in living as the uniquely gifted person you are.
10 The Journey View teaches a person-centered, rather than gift-centered (or ability-centered), understanding of spiritual gifts. We are not focusing on things we get, but who we are. This view is both person-centered and Christocentric because as unique persons, we follow Christ in our journeys of gift development.
11 In terms of salvation, the content and focus for our faith and hope is the atoning death of Christ. But in terms of persevering in running the race of the Christian life, we are directed to the cross-carrying example of how Jesus stayed focused on his mission to go to the cross.
12 See the Gifting Journey worksheet toward the end of the book.

Chapter Ten: Values for Church—Fellowship and Service

1 See Jeffrey Arnold, *The Big Book on Small Groups* (Downers Grove, IL: InterVarsity Press, 1992), 31–33, and Gareth Icenogle, *Biblical Foundations for Small Group Ministry: An Integrative Approach* (Downers Grove, IL: InterVarsity Press, 1994).

2   The inner circle I experienced with my two friends, mentioned at the beginning of chapter 4, is an example of this. Notice that we developed into an inner circle when we decided to not focus on the task of studying a book, but only focus on relational connection. This change in focus, and shrinking of the group to three, made us into an inner circle.
3   This is not to say that there is not an appropriate place for various kinds of classes in local churches. Cognitive learning (of Scripture, skills, doctrine, church history, etc.) can be pursued in classes. But it is in relational groups that cognitive understandings of our Christian faith can be nudged toward application and life change.
4   Interpersonal Communication Programs, Inc. ICP training is now provided through Tyro Support Services, and you can learn more at tyro365.com.
5   In a local church in our area, there is a group that uses their sewing skills to create huggable hearts for persons who have had breast surgeries related to cancer. In a person-centered understanding of spiritual gifts, our interest is not in categorizing what gift these people are using, or associating their sewing skills and dedication of time with one of the listed gifts; instead, it is focused on celebrating and affirming this expression of God's grace in each person. This illustrates the value of having our eyes opened to be looking for creative expressions of gifting in and through our churches. Remember, too, how Rashad's use of his mechanic skills (in chapter 8) became a gift used in ministry.

Chapter Eleven: All People Are Gifted

1   As indicated in chapter 1, I use the phrase "spectrum of grace" to paraphrase Peter's *poikilēs charitos* in 1 Peter 4:10. Peter's discussion of gifts, as also Paul's, are about Christians displaying God's grace through gifts and are certainly referring to the saving grace that has been received by believers. By implying here even unbelievers are part of that spectrum, I am using the phrase loosely. But if the potentials of unbelievers are also God-sourced, we need terminology that recognizes that. Perhaps the easiest way to express it is to reach for the traditional theological category called common grace. Though unbelievers have not experienced God's saving grace, their potentials are certainly evidence of God's grace in creating them with those potentials. Storms, *Understanding Spiritual Gifts*, 319–329. Sam

Storms discusses the issue of whether non-Christians receive spiritual gifts. He concludes that, through common grace, God blesses and, at times, blesses others through unbelievers. Storms's discussion, however, is largely limited to the exercise of miraculous powers.

2   I refer to the popular view's utilitarian understanding of gifts at various places in this book. It is related to this dichotomy between task and being. An endnote in chapter 8 and another in chapter 14 cite examples of this dichotomy in popular view authors.

3   C. S. Lewis, *The Four Loves* (New York: Harcourt Brace Jovanovich, 1960), 17. This is analogous to what Lewis wrote about love: "'Love . . . begins to be a demon the moment he begins to be a god.' This balance seems to me an indispensable safeguard. If we ignore it, the truth that God is love may slyly come to mean for us the converse, that love is God."

Chapter Twelve: Three Views on Gifts

1   Kenneth G. Radant, *Are Our Lifekeys the Right SHAPE for Our Network: Recent Trends in Spiritual Gift Teaching* (Presentation at Evangelical Theological Society 2006 National Meeting. https://www.wordmp3.com/details.aspx?id=7289). One theologian with a special interest in spiritual gifts is Dr. Ken Radant of Carey Theological College in British Columbia. He indicates that a weakness of popular publications on gifts is not paying attention to scholarship related to the relevant scriptures. While this book majors on life application, I seek also to interact with scholarly publications on the topic. That is the case particularly in part 4, and in endnotes throughout. Shortly before publication of this book, Dr. Radant indicated to me that his book, *Grace for Service: An Exegetical Theology of the Spirit's Gifts for Ministry*, will also be published in 2023.

2   Kenneth Berding, *What Are Spiritual Gifts? Rethinking the Conventional View* (Grand Rapids, MI: Kregel Publications, 2006).

3   Charismatics, however, take a decided step away from gifting as mechanical in their emphasis on a significant experiential dimension of receiving and using spiritual gifts. Because of that, not all of my descriptions of the Mechanical View fit them. However, *most of the Mechanical View features I will list are common elements that distinguish popular charismatic and noncharismatic views from the non-mechanical Journey View presented here.* Storms, *Understanding Spiritual Gifts*, 18–21. Sam Storms is a leading charismatic teacher who emphasizes

that gifts are about the Spirit's "presence rather than his presents," thus taking a step away from the mechanical and toward the relational. This is helpful, but (responding to Berding) he classifies himself as still subscribing to the "Traditional View," focusing his definition of gifts on the Spirit's manifestations and impartations to Christians in ways that "exceed the limitations of their finite humanity."

4   Storms, *Understanding Spiritual Gifts*, 47. Another variation is the belief that Spirit baptism happens at conversion, and there is gift-receiving then, but gift-receiving can recur multiple times subsequent to conversion, to a Christian who was already baptized in the Spirit. This is the view of Sam Storms. It often includes the belief that we can and should pursue receiving further spiritual gifts, which is a step away from what I describe as automatic. Such gift-receiving, however, still seems detached from growth status and irrespective of a person's unique identity.

5   Berding, *What Are Spiritual Gifts?*, 7–8. This focus is evident from the beginning in Berding's book: "The central motivation in my writing this book, however, is not related to practical implications for the church, although I'm convinced that these are significant. Rather, my main goal is a biblical one—to understand what Paul always intended to communicate, or not to communicate—about spiritual ministries (and/or abilities)." The amount of space and depth of detailed analysis given to the scriptural data carries his emphasis on careful biblical interpretation from cover to cover.

6   Berding, *What Are Spiritual Gifts?*, 77, 122. "The conventional view of spiritual gifts as abilities disconnects the list passages . . . from the rest of Paul's letters. It does so because Paul doesn't make a Christian's abilities the focus of his discussion anywhere else." He stresses that in 1 Corinthians 12, Romans 12, and Ephesians 4, "Paul doesn't encourage his readers to try to discover their special spiritual abilities; rather, he challenges and encourages them to strengthen the community of faith in whatever roles of ministry that God has placed them."

7   Berding, *What Are Spiritual Gifts?*, 138–140.
8   Berding, *What Are Spiritual Gifts?*, 57–64.
9   Berding, *What Are Spiritual Gifts?*, 145. Numerous times Berding refers to the "so-called spiritual gifts."
10 Berding, *What Are Spiritual Gifts?*, 71–77.
11 Berding, *What Are Spiritual Gifts?*, 32–33.

ENDNOTES

12 Berding, *What Are Spiritual Gifts?*, 199.
13 Berding, *What Are Spiritual Gifts?*, 226–270.
14 Berding, *What Are Spiritual Gifts?*, 192–193.
15 Berding, *What Are Spiritual Gifts?*, 39, 50.
16 Berding, *What Are Spiritual Gifts?*, 139. "Although English usage of the word *gift* presently plays a substantial role in people's assumptions about and acceptance of the conventional view, such usage needs to be once and for all exposed and set aside in future discussions of this topic. The only way to do so successfully in most cases is to steer clear of the use of the word *gift* when discussing the entities that Paul lists in Ephesians 4; Romans 12; and 1 Corinthians 12."
17 Berding, *What Are Spiritual Gifts?*, 145–150. Berding's contextualizations of the gift passages focus on Paul's letters.

Chapter Thirteen: Interpretive Factors

1 It's also the case that the occasion of an Epistle can vary in specificity. In Romans and Ephesians, as I note elsewhere, Paul is not responding to specific church situations at the level he is in 1 Corinthians. The occasion of Romans and Ephesians may have more to do with Paul's general convictions about what believers need to grasp, while he is responding especially to specific problems in Corinth.
2 Osborne, *The Hermeneutical Spiral*, 256.
3 When I speak of these "clues" and "biblical threads," I am referring to "canonical connections," which I address under that name elsewhere in this chapter and book.
4 https://www.merriam-webster.com/dictionary/reify. I first learned of reification through a DMin class with Dr. Warren Heard. He taught that we need to be careful not to reify concepts not intended to be concrete, using as one example "old man" and "new man." Warren J. Heard, Ph.D., Notes by Bill Smart in Heard's class "An Integration of Theology and Psychology" (1994), 16b. Reification, in and of itself, is not always erroneous. It becomes an error (a misinterpretation) if the intent of words is conceptual or metaphorical, as I believe is the case with gifting language.
5 Osborne, *The Hermeneutical Spiral*, 104–105. Dr. Osborne also speaks of "dead metaphors," wherein "the image has become an idiom, understood directly by the hearer without producing a word-picture in the mind." He cautions that "the interpreter can read too much into a dead metaphor by erroneously stressing its picture value." I

believe that this has happened, in the popular view's interpretation of *charismata* when translated as *gifts*.
6   Don J. Payne, Ph.D., in an email to me, 10/25/22. Though he did not speak of misinterpreting the gifting metaphor, Dr. Payne sees reification in the popular understanding of gifts: "The subtle, undetected, and often problematic Thomistic underpinnings of much evangelical thinking about spiritual gifts is that gifts have a sort of existence or ontology of their own, somewhat like Aquinas and late Medieval Roman Catholicism seemed to understand grace in substantive terms rather than in terms of divine relationship and presence."
7   Osborne, *The Hermeneutical Spiral*, 300.
8   Don J. Payne, PhD, in an email to me, 10/25/22. See appendix 3 for further thoughts on interdisciplinary integration on this issue.
9   In listing these metaphors, I am including words used by Paul or Peter (body, gift, varied) as well as broader metaphors I derive through canonical connections. The former conform to the characteristics of ancient metaphor Osborne describes. The latter function as broader prototypes for life application.
10 The metaphor of God as the Divine Warrior is also relevant, as I've noted in relation to the spoils metaphor, particularly as we've seen it applied to Christ (and gift-giving) in Ephesians. Tremper Longman III and Daniel G. Reid, *God is a Warrior*, Studies in Old Testament Biblical Theology, eds. Willem A. VanGemeren and Tremper Longman III (Grand Rapids, MI: Zondervan Publishing House, 1995). Longman and Reid present the full scriptural panorama of this metaphor for God's relationship with his people.
11 Class notes by this author, "Hermeneutics and Homiletics" (D. A. Carson, PhD, 1992), 3.
12 Don J. Payne, *Already Sanctified: A Theology of the Christian Life in Light of God's Completed Work* (Grand Rapids, MI: Baker Academic, 2020). We could use the term "sanctification" instead of growth, with progressive sanctification in view. It's up to you if you would like to use that terminology. However, I've recently been influenced by Dr. Don Payne's *Already Sanctified*, where he develops the argument that Scripture's dominant and controlling emphasis regarding sanctification is its accomplished reality. He sees transformation and growth as flowing out of that but makes the case for a different perspective on sanctification.

ENDNOTES

Chapter Fourteen: Romans & Ephesians

1. For the meanings of *dokimazo,* see Bauer's *Greek Lexicon:* Walter Bauer, *A Greek-English Lexicon of the New Testament and Other Early Christian Literature,* translated by William F. Arndt and F. Wilbur Gingrich (Chicago: University of Chicago Press, 1957), 201.
2. Implied by John Wesley in his Romans commentary (John Wesley, "Romans," in *The Classic Bible Commentary,* ed. Owen Collins (Wheaton, IL: Crossway Books, 1999), 1210). Also indicated by Friesen in his book on God's will (Garry Friesen, *Decision Making and the Will of God: A Biblical Alternative to the Traditional View* (Portland, OR: Multnomah Press, 1980), 106–108).
3. I explained and argued earlier for a metaphorical interpretation of gifting, and am therefore assuming it here.
4. T. K. Abbott, "A Critical and Exegetical Commentary on the Epistles to the Ephesians and to the Colossians," in *The International Critical Commentary on the Holy Scriptures of the Old and New Testaments,* eds. Samuel R. Driver and Charles A. Briggs (Edinburgh: T & T Clark, 1977), i–ix.
5. See my comments on "occasion and theology" in chapter 13.
6. Popular view proponents often make 1 Corinthians central and the other gift passages secondary. That's an interpretive decision, and I think there is a better argument, as presented here, for the centrality of the Ephesians (and Romans) gift passages. I would not call 1 Corinthians secondary, but say it's more situationally influenced.
7. Storms, *Understanding Spiritual Gifts,* xv–xvi. Storms writes, "Gifts are to fruit what means are to ends." He sees individual and corporate growth as the goal, and gifts as instrumental toward the goal.
8. Longman and Reid, *God is a Warrior,* 138, 152, 156–157. See Longman and Reid's connection of Ephesians 6:10–18 with the cosmic battle being waged following Christ.
9. Timothy G. Gombis, "Cosmic Lordship and Divine Gift-Giving: Psalm 68 in Ephesians 4:8," *Novum Testamentum,* vol. 4, fasc. 4 (2005), 367–380. Accessed 8/23/22, https://www.jstor.org/stable/25442460. Gombis presents a convincing contextualized interpretation of Ephesians 4:8. He a) demonstrates that the imagery of divine warfare (as understood in the ancient Near East and the Old Testament) is significant in Ephesians, seen particularly in Ephesians 1 and 2, and then in 4:8–10; b) sees the focus in 4:7–10 as on Christ as the victorious and ascending Divine Warrior; c) understands Paul's

change of verbs ("gave gifts" instead of "receiving gifts") as indicating Paul's appropriation of the whole narrative movement of Psalm 68; d) interprets "the lower parts of the earth" (4:10) as indicating Christ's grave, i.e. his death; and e) refutes the interpretation that identifies this descent of Christ with the Spirit's descent at Pentecost. Gombis's interpretations accord well with several aspects of the Journey View. He weaves a fascinating picture that sets the giving of spiritual gifts in a cosmic context, far from our normal utilitarian and non-imaginative focus. He does not develop further any gifts-as-spoils application; his focus is instead on interpretation of specific texts.

10 Richard A. Taylor, *Bibliotheca Sacra* 148, no. 591 (Jul–Sep 1991): 319–322. The use of the Old Testament in the New is an area of considerable scholarly debate, including among evangelicals. Beyond that, Paul's verb change in his citation of Psalm 68:18 is also subject to conflicting views. And even beyond that, some scholars have felt that Psalm 68 is the most difficult of all the psalms to interpret! Thus, the avoidance of Ephesians 4:8–10 by the vast majority of popular view teachers on gifts is perhaps understandable. But the verses could not have been placed by Paul in a more integral place in his teaching about gifts in Ephesians, leading to the obvious question: What has the popular view missed? (See more thoughts on this subject toward the end of appendix 2.)

11 See my use of this idea in Psalm 68 in chapter 2. Longman and Reid, *God is a Warrior*, 150–151. Note also Longman and Reid's setting of Ephesians 4:8–9 in the context of divine warfare as portrayed in Ephesians and connected with Christ's gift-giving.

12 D. Moody Smith, "The Pauline literature," *It Is Written: Scripture Citing Scripture*, 281. In this quote, Smith is translating Swiss theologian Ulrich Luz. I do not take this quote to mean that understanding the Old Testament in and of itself is unimportant. Rather that Paul's *first* concern when citing it to Christians was to bring to them the Old Testament's insight concerning the topic at hand.

13 Various explanations are offered: Colin Brown, "Heaven, Ascend, Above," in *The New International Dictionary of New Testament Theology*, ed. Colin Brown (Grand Rapids: Zondervan, 1976), 2:186-187). Brown feels the two verses are "in contrast," needing explanation. John Calvin, *Calvin's Commentaries. Galatians, Ephesians, Philippians, Colossians, 1 & 2 Thessalonians, 1 & 2 Timothy, Titus,*

Philemon: Commentaries on the Epistles of Paul to the Galatians and Ephesians, trans. William Pringle (Grand Rapids, MI: Baker, 1989), vol. 21, 273–274). Calvin acknowledges that "since . . . the intention of *receiving* was to *give* gifts, Paul can hardly be said to have departed from the substance, whatever alteration there may be in the words." But then he suggests that after *aichmalōsian* Paul adds "his own language . . ." Max Wilcox, "Text Form," in *It is Written: Scripture Citing Scripture: Essays in Honour of Barnabas Lindars,* eds. D. A. Carson and H. G. M. Williamson (Cambridge: University Press, 1988), 198–199. Then there are those who see Paul using a variant source, as Wilcox points out. For even more options, see Taylor, "The Use of Psalm 68:18 in Ephesians 4:8 in Light of the Ancient Versions," 319–336.

14 Gombis, "Cosmic Lordship," 374. Commenting on the psalm's use in 4:8, Gombis writes, "Psalm 68 . . . depicts Yahweh conquering his enemies and then blessing his people with gifts." Kidner, *Tyndale Old Testament Commentaries,* 14a:242. Kidner seems to agree with my point that the gifts in Psalm 68 are spoils, though he uses different terms: "Who are these captives, and whose are the gifts? The battle imagery and the echoes of the Song of Deborah indicate enemy prisoners and enemy reparations. God has won His war, entered His capital and put *the rebellious* under tribute." Delitzsch, 253–256. With Delitzsch, I see at least one image, in 68:13–14, of the people enriched with spoils given to them by the King: a dove shimmering with silver and gold, and perhaps also the dark hill of Zalmon littered (like sparkling snow) with the fallen kings and their riches.

15 Commentators who clarify the relation of the gift-giving in Ephesians 4 with that in Psalm 68 include: Kidner, *Tyndale Old Testament Commentaries,* 14a:242, who writes that 4:8 ". . . summarizes rather than contradicts the psalm, whose next concern is with the blessings God dispenses [after first receiving them]," as well as Delitzsch, cited earlier in a chapter 2 endnote.

16 The third mentioned option, Christ's descent to earth, is a reference to his incarnation. A refinement on that view is that his descent is to the grave (i.e., a reference to his death). Yet another variation on all these options is the once popular view that Christ descended into hell between his death and resurrection. In recent history, the two favored options seem to be the identification of Christ's descent with the Spirit's descent at Pentecost versus the descent as his incarnation,

perhaps especially his death. (W. Hall Harris III, "The Ascent and Descent of Christ in Ephesians 4:9–10," *Bibliotheca Sacra* 151, (April-June 1994): 198–214) Harris strongly and with extensive exegetical and historical detail argues the former. (Gombis, "Cosmic Lordship.") However, Gombis rebuts the various points in Harris' view, understanding the descent as referring to Christ's death and seeing Divine Warrior imagery manifested in the triumphant ascending Christ.

17 Gombis, "Cosmic Lordship," 373. In agreeing with Gombis on this point, I am saying that if we see 4:8 as importing the whole movement of Psalm 68 and its "imagery of divine warfare" into Ephesians 4:7-10, then we should understand the descent as related to battles and preceding the victorious ascent.

Chapter Fifteen: 1 Corinthians & 1 Peter

1 Carson, *Showing the Spirit*, 23. Carson points out that Paul switches from *pneumatika* to *charismata* to "lay emphasis on grace."
2 It is not that Paul is saying that *pneumatika* is a worldly way to describe expressions of people's gifts. It is the Corinthians' fascination with *pneumatika* that partakes of worldly wisdom, with its attendant consequences. Paul will use both *charismata* and *pneumatika* to refer to spiritual gifts, but he sees that the emphasis on grace in and through each person, brought to the forefront in *charismata*, is more necessary for the Corinthians and us.
3 It is likely that we should understand these categories like a Venn diagram or a continuum, in which they overlap or blend into one another. This is similar to how we are interpreting the gift categories in this book. Throughout, we are talking about people with their varied gift expressions.
4 In 12:28 Paul lists eight gifts. But when he reprises that list in question form, in 12:29–30, he leaves some of those out and adds a ninth.
5 Carson, *Showing the Spirit*, 36.
6 Carson, *Showing the Spirit*. The first two points are from page 35, the third from page 37, and the fourth from page 40.
7 *Poikilos* occurs only ten times in the NT. Three times it refers to various diseases healed by Jesus (Matt. 4:24; Mk. 1:34; Lk. 4:40), twice to various sinful lusts (2 Tim. 3:6; Tit. 3:3), twice to trials in life (Jam. 1:2; 1 Pet. 1:6), once to a variety of miracles (Heb. 2:4), once

to varying strange doctrines (Heb. 13:9), and once to God's grace (1 Pet. 4:10). *Polupoikilos* occurs just once, modifying God's wisdom (Eph. 3:10). Thus, eight of the uses are negative, three positive. Due to this sparse usage in the NT, it is important to consult extrabiblical evidence for a broader understanding of the word, which I have done and documented in a chapter 1 endnote. I have emphasized that its use in 1 Peter 4 and Ephesians 3 points to the beauty and wonder of the diversity of God's people, and I see that as well founded on this survey of its extrabiblical use.

8 I use the illustration variously. Previously, I spoke of God's grace (and wisdom) as the prism, here I speak of the prism as refracting God's grace and wisdom. The biblical input is *poikilos* as a descriptor of God's grace and wisdom. The human illustration can vary.

9 In preaching and teaching, I have illustrated God's variegated spectrum of grace as a stained-glass window that pictures Christ. We are each a pane in that window. I use the homophone of "pane and pain" to point to how our trials/battles are necessary for each of us to develop into the unique hue we are as we together display Jesus.

10 This is the case in the popular view, even when the caveat is added that any list is not exhaustive.

Chapter Sixteen: Categories vs Uniqueness

1 Some schools of thought in psychology see each person as unique, and some do not. Scripture does not dwell on the theme of individual uniqueness. The creation account does not require it. Neither do Psalm 139 nor the "hairs of your head" passages (Matthew 10:30; Luke 12:7). The apostle John seems to come closest. In John 10:3, the shepherd "calls his own sheep by name," sheep with whom he has a mutual *knowing* relationship (10:14); and the verse we have emphasized here, Revelation 2:17, where we learn that each overcomer will receive "a new name . . . that no one knows except the one who receives it." We are probably meant to regard this issue as more a relational question than a scientific one. We are called to ascribe to one another a preciousness that fits best with understanding each person as unique. This leads to the attending *agape* we have earlier discussed.

2 See comments on resources for development under "Well Worth Fighting" in chapter 6.

3 Lewis, *The Weight of Glory*, 18.

4   Benner, *The Gift of Being Yourself*, 17. "We should never be tempted to think that growth in Christlikeness reduces our uniqueness. While some Christian visions of the spiritual life imply that as we become more like Christ we look more and more like each other, such a cultic expectation of loss of individuality has nothing in common with genuine Christian spirituality. Paradoxically, as we become more and more like Christ we become more uniquely our own true self."

Chapter Seventeen: Manifestations of the Spirit

1   In this book I argue that our understanding of spiritual gifts should focus on Jesus rather than the Spirit. This is neither to deny that spiritual gifts manifest the Spirit, nor is it to downplay the pervasive and powerful work of the Spirit in all aspects of our lives. That work is the subject of scores of biblical texts, making it important for our understanding. Yet this is a book about spiritual gifts in particular, and I believe the Spirit's role with respect to gifts has been misconstrued by the popular view while Christ's role has been minimized. The role of the Spirit in our salvation and growth is pervasive and essential. In the Journey View, the baptism of the Spirit at salvation, which initiates his indwelling presence in the believer, is the most strategic step in gift development.
2   John 14:16–18, 26; 15:26; 16:7–15; Acts 1:4–8.
3   Peter's sermon at Pentecost in Acts 2 is the premier example of this. On this day, in which the powerful reality of the Spirit's descent upon believers (2:1–4) is the big event (along with the salvation of three thousand!), Peter moves the focus to Jesus Christ. In the many gospel presentations in the book of Acts, this emphasis on Jesus is repeated.
4   Berding, *What Are Spiritual Gifts?*, 162–163. Berding indicates that, except in the early section of 1 Corinthians 12, the Spirit is not emphasized in the gift passages. He sees that Paul's emphasis on the Spirit focuses on other themes: "The somewhat light use of explicit references to the Holy Spirit in some of these ministry passages [his term for the gift passages] would not be noticeable were it not for Paul's insistence on mentioning the Holy Spirit in so many other passages throughout his letters. Clearly, the focal point of Paul's discussion of the Holy Spirit is not the so-called spiritual gifts but is the work of the Holy Spirit in salvation and sanctification."
5   I will generally use the term "supernatural gifts" rather than charismatic gifts. As many authors writing on gifts point out,

ENDNOTES

charismata is a term that covers all spiritual gifts in the Epistles. But some involve miraculous manifestations, and those I'm referring to here as supernatural. I could have also used "miraculous." Storms, *The Beginner's Guide to Spiritual Gifts*, 15–16. Sam Storms, a prominent charismatic pastor and author today, uses the terms supernatural and miraculous of these gifts.

6   Acts 2:1–11; 10:44–48; 19:1–7. Cf. 8:14–17; 11:15–18; 15:6–9.
7   Acts 3:1–10; 5:12–16; 8:4–8; 9:32–42; 14:8–10; 19:11–12; 20:9–12; 28:7–9.
8   It is my view that, in the gift list in 12:8–11, there is a mixture of supernatural and non-supernatural gifts. Whether that is correct or not, though, it is not generally disputed that Paul is intending his readers to know that all the kinds of gifts are manifestations of the Spirit.
9   There are important theological, biblical, and practical issues in the debates between charismatics and noncharismatics. I just don't think, if our topic is understanding spiritual gifts, that those issues are most important. In presenting the Journey View, I am presenting what I think the Scriptures point to as most important in understanding spiritual gifting.

Worksheet 1: Agape Evaluation

1   In chapter 11 we focused on how unbelievers can also be on the journey of growth and gifting. You can use the features of love considered in the Agape Evaluation as a guide to offering such love to your unbelieving friends.

Worksheet 2: The Gifting Journey

1   We've earlier noted that unbelievers can be on that journey also. But it is our salvation, and the coming of God's Spirit to live in us, that is a beginning of our gifting journeys in the power of the Spirit.

Appendix 2: The Spoils Theme

1   This interpretation is supported by Gombis in "Cosmic Lordship," referred to previously in chapter 14 endnotes. Gombis goes on to specify Christ's descent as focusing on a subset of the incarnation, i.e., his grave. That may be correct, but I emphasize that Christ's struggles (against opposition) leading up to his grave are also relevant to Paul's intent in 4:9–10.

2   David L. Larsen, *Telling the Old, Old Story: The Art of Narrative Preaching* (Wheaton, IL: Crossway, 1995), 18–31. Larsen points out the problems and dangers of excessive fascination with narrative, which can lead to the absence of any propositional theology. At the same time, that author's goal is to draw evangelicals into a proper and beneficial use of biblical story, bringing balance to our previous neglect of narrative.

Appendix 3: Integration Issues

1   Class notes by this author, "An Integration of Theology and Psychology," (Warren J. Heard, PhD, July 1994), 1b. Dr. Heard clarified for me the distinctions between Thomistic and Augustinian integrations in the DMin class I took with him.
2   See earlier comments, in chapter 13 under Use of Metaphor, on the influence of reification and Thomistic thinking on our doctrine of spiritual gifts.

REFERENCE LIST

Abbott, T. K. "A Critical and Exegetical Commentary on the Epistles to the Ephesians and to the Colossians," in *The International Critical Commentary on the Holy Scriptures of the Old and New Testaments*, edited by Samuel R. Driver and Charles A. Briggs. Edinburgh: T & T Clark, 1977.

Abbott-Smith, G. *A Manual Greek Lexicon of the New Testament*. Edinburgh: T. & T. Clark, 1968.

Allender, Dan B. *To Be Told: God Invites You to Coauthor Your Future*. Colorado Springs, CO: WaterBrook Press, 2005.

Arnold, Jeffrey. *The Big Book on Small Groups*. Downers Grove, IL: InterVarsity Press, 1992.

Baird, Christopher S. "Science Questions with Surprising Answers." Accessed November 3, 2021. https://www.wtamu.edu/~cbaird/sq/2012/12/04/why-are-there-only-six-fundamental-colors-red-orange-yellow-green-blue-and-violet/.

Bauer, Walter. *A Greek-English Lexicon of the New Testament and Other Early Christian Literature*, translated by William F. Arndt and F. Wilbur Gingrich. Chicago: University of Chicago Press, 1957.

Benner, David G. *Psychotherapy and the Spiritual Quest*. Grand Rapids: Baker, 1988.

Benner, David G. *The Gift of Being Yourself: The Sacred Call to Self-Discovery* (Expanded Edition). Downers Grove, IL: InterVarsity Press, (Kindle Edition) 2015.

Berding, Kenneth. *What Are Spiritual Gifts? Rethinking the Conventional View*. Grand Rapids, MI: Kregel Publications, 2006.

Brown, Colin. "Heaven, Ascend, Above," in *The New International Dictionary of New Testament Theology*, edited by Colin Brown. Grand Rapids, MI: Zondervan, 1976.

Bugbee, Bruce, and Don Cousins, and Bill Hybels. *Network: The Right People in the Right Places for the Right Reasons—Leader's Guide.* Grand Rapids: Zondervan, 1994.

Bugbee, Bruce, and Don Cousins, and Bill Hybels. *Network: The Right People in the Right Places for the Right Reasons—Participant's Guide.* Grand Rapids: Zondervan, 1994.

Calvin, John. *Calvin's Commentaries. Galatians, Ephesians, Philippians, Colossians, 1 & 2 Thessalonians, 1 & 2 Timothy, Titus, Philemon: Commentaries on the Epistles of Paul to the Galatians and Ephesians*, translated by William Pringle, vol. 21. Grand Rapids: Baker, 1989.

Carson, D. A. *Showing the Spirit: A Theological Exposition of 1 Corinthians 12–14.* Grand Rapids: Baker Book House, 1987.

Crabb, Larry J. *Connecting: Healing for Ourselves and Our Relationships, a Radical New Vision.* Nashville: Word, 1997.

Crabb, Larry. *Soul Talk: The Language God Longs for Us to Speak.* Brentwood, TN: Integrity Publishers, 2003.

Curtis, Brent, and John Eldredge. *The Sacred Romance: Drawing Closer to the Heart of God.* Nashville: Thomas Nelson, Inc., 1997.

Eulexis-web, Baobab. "Poikilos." Accessed November 2, 2021. https://outils.biblissima.fr/fr/eulexis-web/?lemma=%CF%80%CE%BF%CE%B9%CE%BA%CE%B9%CE%BB%CE%BF%CF%82&dict=LSJ.

Ford, Paul R. *Unleash Your Church!: A Comprehensive Strategy to Help People Discover and Use Their Spiritual Gifts.* Pasadena, CA: Charles E. Fuller Institute, 1993.

Friesen, Garry. *Decision Making and the Will of God: A Biblical Alternative to the Traditional View.* Portland, OR: Multnomah Press, 1980.

Gombis, Timothy G. "Cosmic Lordship and Divine Gift-Giving: Psalm 68 in Ephesians 4:8." *Novum Testamentum,* vol. 4, Fasc. 4 (2005): 367-380. Accessed August 23, 2022. https://www.jstor.org/stable/25442460.

Harris III, W. Hall. "The Ascent and Descent of Christ in Ephesians 4:9–10." *Bibliotheca Sacra* 151, (April–June 1994): 198–214.

Heard, Jr., Warren J. "Eschatologically Oriented Psychology: A New Paradigm for the Integration of Psychology and Christianity." In *God and Culture: Essays in Honor of Carl F. H. Henry,* edited by D. A. Carson and John D. Woodbridge, 106–133. Grand Rapids. MI: William B. Eerdmans Publishing, 1993.

Hestenes, Roberta. *Building Christian Community Through Small Groups.* Pasadena, CA: Fuller Seminary Bookstore, 1985.

Icenogle, Gareth. *Biblical Foundations for Small Group Ministry: An Integrative Approach.* Downers Grove, IL: InterVarsity Press, 1994.

Keil, C. F., and F. Delitzsch. *Commentary on the Old Testament,* translated by Francis Bolton. Volume 5:2, *Psalms,* by F. Delitzsch. Grand Rapids: Eerdmans, 1975, original edition, 1871.

Kidner, Derek. *Psalms 1–72: An Introduction and Commentary.* In the *Tyndale Old Testament Commentaries,* edited by D.J. Wiseman, vol. 14a. Downers Grove, Ill: InterVarsity Press, 1973.

Larsen, David L. *Telling the Old, Old Story: The Art of Narrative Preaching.* Wheaton, IL: Crossway, 1995.

Lewis, C. S. *The Four Loves.* New York: Harcourt Brace Jovanovich, 1960.

Lewis, C. S. *The Lion, the Witch and the Wardrobe.* In The Chronicles of Narnia, vol. 2. New York: HarperCollins, 1950.

Lewis, C. S. *The Screwtape Letters*. New York: Macmillan, 1942. Reprint, 1961.

Lewis, C. S. *The Weight of Glory: And Other Addresses*. New York: Macmillan Publishing Co., 1949.

Longman III, Tremper, and Daniel G. Reid. *God is a Warrior*. In Studies in Old Testament Biblical Theology, edited by Willem A. VanGemeren and Tremper Longman III. Grand Rapids, MI: Zondervan Publishing House (Kindle edition), 1995.

Merriam-Webster.com. "Reify." Accessed on August 21, 2022. https://www.merriam-webster.com/dictionary/reify.

Merton, Thomas. "Learning to Live." In *Love and Living*, edited by Naomi Burton Stone and Patrick Hart, 3–14. Orlando: Harcourt Brace, 1979.

Metaxas, Eric. *Bonhoeffer: Pastor, Martyr, Prophet, Spy*. Nashville: Thomas Nelson, 2010.

Miller, Sherod, and Phyllis Miller. *Core Communication: Maps, Skills, and Processes*. Evergreen, CO: Interpersonal Communication Programs, Inc., 2011.

Moon, Gary W. *Homesick for Eden: A Soul's Journey to Joy*. Ann Arbor, MI: Servant Publications, 1997.

Moulton, James Hope, and George Milligan. *The Vocabulary of the Greek Testament: Illustrated from the Papyri and Other Non-Literary Sources*. Grand Rapids, MI: Eerdmans, 1930 (Reprinted 1982).

Oertli, Ronald B. *Right Fit: Discover Who You Are and Where You Fit*. Littleton, CO: Stepstones, 1996.

Osborne, Grant R. *The Hermeneutical Spiral: A Comprehensive Introduction to Interpretation*. Downers Grove, IL: InterVarsity Press, 1991.

REFERENCE LIST

Payne, Don J. *Already Sanctified: A Theology of the Christian Life in Light of God's Completed Work.* Grand Rapids: Baker Academic, 2020.

Peterson, Eugene. *Working the Angles: The Shape of Pastoral Integrity.* Grand Rapids: Eerdmans, 1987.

Radant, Kenneth G. *Are Our Lifekeys the Right SHAPE for Our Network: Recent Trends in Spiritual Gift Teaching.* Presentation at Evangelical Theological Society 2006 National Meeting. https://www.wordmp3.com/details.aspx?id=7289.

Sabourin, Leopold. *The Psalms: Their Origin and Meaning.* New York: Alba House, 1974.

Smith, D. Moody. "The Pauline literature." In *It Is Written: Scripture Citing Scripture: Essays in Honour of Barnabas Lindars*, edited by D. A. Carson and H. G. M. Williamson, 265–291. Cambridge: University Press, 1988.

Snyder, Howard A. *The Problem of Wineskins: Church Structure in a Technological Age.* Downers Grove, IL: InterVarsity Press, 1975.

Storms, Sam. *The Beginner's Guide to Spiritual Gifts.* Bloomington, MN: Bethany House Publishers, 2012.

Storms, Sam. *Understanding Spiritual Gifts.* Grand Rapids: Zondervan (Kindle edition), 2020.

Taylor, Richard A. "The Use of Psalm 68:18 in Ephesians 4:8 in Light of the Ancient Versions." *Bibliotheca Sacra* 148, no. 591 (Jul–Sep 1991): 319–336.

United Bible Societies. *The Greek New Testament.* 3d edition, edited by Kurt Aland, Matthew Black, Carlo M. Martini, Bruce M. Metzger, and Allen Wikgren. New York: American Bible Society, 1975.

Wagner, C. Peter. *Your Spiritual Gifts Can Help Your Church Grow.* Ventura, CA: Regal Books, 1979.

Wesley, John. "Romans." In *The Classic Bible Commentary*, edited by Owen Collins. Wheaton, IL: Crossway Books, 1999.

Wilcox, Max. "Text Form." In *It is Written: Scripture Citing Scripture: Essays in Honour of Barnabas Lindars*, edited by D. A. Carson and H. G. M. Williamson, 193-204. Cambridge: University Press, 1988.

Wordspring Music LLC, Meaux Jeaux Music, Da Bears Da Bears Da Bears Music, Tony Wood Songs. "Fearless." Sung by Jasmine Murray.

ABOUT THE AUTHOR

BILL SMART was a pastor for 20 years, serving in associate roles in Ohio and Kansas, and as a senior pastor in Missouri. He then served 15 years as a hospice chaplain, during which he and his wife (a counseling psychologist) led a personal growth workshop and marriage retreats.

Bill's passion is to support people in learning to authentically relate to God, self, and others. He began questioning the popular view of spiritual gifts during seminary, and his studies led him to an understanding of gifts that focuses on your journey: growing into the unique you God created. Its themes have bled through in his ministries to people throughout his various career roles.

Together Bill and Susan count 6 children and 14 grandchildren, enjoying connection with them during their retirement. Bill is a graduate of Dallas Theological Seminary (ThM) and Trinity Evangelical Divinity School (DMin).

Find Bill online at www.BillSmartAuthor.com, where you can read his blogs and sign up to receive email notices of future blogs.

And on Facebook: Bill Smart, Author